The Civil War Era
and the Lower Rio Grande Valley:
a Brief History

The Civil War Era and the Lower Rio Grande Valley: a Brief History

Rolando Avila

Introduction by Christopher L. Miller

Foreword by Patricia Alvarez McHatton

Community Historical Archaeology Project with Schools Program
The University of Texas Rio Grande Valley

2018

Copyright © 2018 The University of Texas Rio Grande Valley on behalf of the Community Historical Archaeology Project with Schools Program

All rights reserved. This book or any portion thereof may not be reproduced or used in any manner whatsoever without the express written permission of the publisher except for the use of brief quotations in a book review or scholarly journal.

First Printing: 2018

ISBN 978-0-9982070-3-2

Published by UTRGV's Community Historical Archaeology Project with Schools Program

1201 W University Drive
Edinburg, TX 78539

www.utrgv.edu/chaps

Dedication

To my Teachers.

Contents

List of Figures ix

Acknowledgements x

Foreword: Patricia Alvarez McHatton xi

Preface xiii

Introduction: Christopher L. Miller 1

Chapter 1: On the Road to Civil War (1836-1860) 5

Chapter 2: Early Civil War Years (1861-1862) 23

Chapter 3: Late Civil War Years (1863-1865) 39

Chapter 4: Reconstruction (1866-1877) 53

Chronology 65

Appendix I: Russell K. Skowronek 67

Appendix II: County Maps 73

Further Reading 79

Index 83

About the Author 85

List of Figures

Figure 01.01 Sam Houston
Figure 01.02 Porfirio Diaz
Figure 01.03 Congressman Abraham Lincoln
Figure 01.04 Juan Nepomuceno Cortina courtesy of Jerry D Thompson
Figure 01.05 Richard King courtesy of King Ranch Archives
Figure 01.06 Wooden structures at Ringgold Barracks courtesy of Rio Grande City CISD
Figure 01.07 Abraham Lincoln c. 1861
Figure 02.01 John Salmon "Rip" Ford
Figure 02.02 Confederate Colonel John S. Ford
courtesy DeGolyer Library at Southern Methodist University
Figure 02.03 Cotton Trails Map by Tom A. Fort, Museum of South Texas History
Figure 02.04 Benito Juarez/Emperor Maximillian (Library of Congress)
Figure 02.05 Map of Bagdad Mexico
courtesy of Museums of Port Isabel
Figure 02.06 Engraving of bustling Bagdad, Mexico 1864-1865
courtesy of the Brownsville Historical Association
Figure 03.01 Plan of the 1846 Fort Brown (US National Archives)
Figure 03.02 Colonel Santos Benavides courtesy of Webb County Heritage Foundation
Figure 03.03 Zacate Creek view from south to north
Figure 03.04 Confederate Soldiers from Laredo, TX
courtesy of Webb County Historical Foundation
Figure 03.05 Battle at Palmito Ranch painting by Clara Lily Ely,
courtesy Texas Southmost College
Figure 03.06 Private John Jefferson Williams (US Army Military Institute)
Figure 04.01 Fort McIntosh US Military Reservation 1892 37
Figure 04.02 Flag representing 84th US Colored Infantry
courtesy of Behring Center - Smithsonian Institution
Figure 04.03 Buffalo Soldiers by Frederick Remington
Figure 04.04 Rio Grande Valley Civil War Trail highway sign

Acknowledgements

We would like to thank our sponsors. This book would not have been possible without support from the Community Historical Archaeology Project with Schools (CHAPS) Program, the School of Interdisciplinary Programs and Community Engagement, the College of Liberal Arts at the University of Texas Rio Grande Valley, the Houston Endowment for Civic Engagement, the Summerlee Foundation, the Summerfield G. Roberts Foundation of Dallas, Palo Alto National Historic Park, National Park Service, Texas Historical Commission, THE STUDIO@UTRGV, and the Rio Grande Valley Civil War Trail.

Foreword: Patricia Alvarez McHatton

As a recent transplant to the Rio Grande Valley, I can't help but recall an early conversation that took place during my interview for founding dean of the College of Education and P-16 Integration at The University of Texas Rio Grande Valley. I was asked if I had ever been to South Texas. I shared that in fact the closest I had been to South Texas was Austin. The individual then responded, "well then you get the job as you are the only person we have spoken to that knows Austin isn't South Texas." We had a hearty laugh, but I am constantly amazed at the reality that many folks do not know a lot about South Texas, or if they do, they have a flawed perspective of what living in the region is like.

It is for this reason that the work of Drs. Miller and Skowronek is so important. The Community Historical Archaeology Project with Schools (CHAPS) is comprised of faculty from varied disciplines, community members, and other key stakeholders. Its' mission is to further a deep understanding of the historical significance of South Texas. A major initiative was the development of the first Civil War Trail in Texas. This work makes available to teachers a treasure trove of educational resources including memorabilia from the civil war era and a series of lesson plans aligned to the Texas Essential Knowledge and Skills standards. Further, the Civil War Trail website contains additional resources including audio tours in both English and Spanish. Providing resources in both languages demonstrates a commitment to valuing the individuals that reside in the region, many of whose native language is Spanish.

The current volume by Dr. Avila builds upon this past rich foundation by deepening understanding of South Texas' role in the Civil War. It provides information foundational to the history of the civil war era in the region and situates the region as integral to the development of the nation. More importantly, it provides students with an historical accounting that they have not necessarily been privy to. Embedded in the text are excerpts from the UTRGV Civil War Trail, bringing to life historical figures from the region and showcasing locations known by those of us living in the area.

For me, as an educator whose teaching philosophy is focused on empowering children and youth to become active participants in shaping the world they live in, I applaud the emphasis on place-based education to foster engagement between school and community. It is through such exploration that students can learn to read the world and their role in it. This text provides a concise history of the role the lower Rio Grande Valley played during the civil war era. Hopefully, it will serve as a launching pad for readers to continue discovering the contributions of the region within and beyond Texas.

Patricia Alvarez McHatton
Executive Vice President for Academic Affairs, Student Success, and P-16 Integration
The University of Texas Rio Grande Valley

Preface

The Rio Grande Valley Civil War Trail was conceived during the sesquicentennial of the American Civil War by a consortium of local historians and museum specialists in Deep South Texas in conjunction with the Community Historical Archeology Project in Schools (CHAPS) program at the University of Texas Rio Grande Valley (UTRGV). The 200-mile long trail stretches from Laredo to Brownsville. Along the trail, some sixty sites tell the story of the war and its associated personalities. Information on these sites and the trail in general may be found on the Civil War Trail website (www.utrgv.edu/civilwar-trail).

This book provides an overview of this tumultuous era. Those seeking more details may consult the sources listed in the Further Reading list at the end of this book. Those teaching this era may consult the RGV Civil War Trail lesson plans available on the Civil War Trail website and at the UTRGV CHAPS program.

In closing, the UTRGV CHAPS Program encourages the community to travel the trail and enjoy the historic landscape. However, the CHAPS Program would also like to advise visitors not to collect artifacts or in any way disturb the integrity of historic sites.

Rolando Avila
Lecturer, History
The University of Texas Rio Grande Valley

Introduction: Christopher L. Miller

In a recent book review Hannah Blubaugh (Miami University of Ohio) observed that there have been over fifty thousand books and pamphlets published about the Civil War since its inception. Yet here I find myself writing an introduction to another such book. The question must surely arise: why? Why yet another Civil War history book? The answer to this will become apparent to the reader as s/he wades into the volume at hand. Yes, this is another Civil War history book, but it deals with an aspect of the Civil War that does not appear—even as an aside or footnote—in the vast majority of those other fifty thousand books and pamphlets. This is the untold story of the complicated cross-border, multi-sided civil war era specific to the Rio Grande Valley in both Texas and Mexico that took place most intensively between 1861 and 1867, yet the roots of which reach back to at least 1846 and extend forward to at least 1877.

This book has grown out of a project that was initially conceived back in 2012 when two professors at what then was the University of Texas—Pan American, Russell Skowronek and I, were in a darkened office chatting about the promise of public history in the Rio Grande Valley. We recognized that we were just entering the second year of the sesquicentennial observations of the American Civil War. Oddly, Texas, which has capitalized on its Civil War heritage in so many ways, was one of the few participant states that did not have a trail devoted specifically to the American Civil War. We then set out to rectify that situation.

With the aid of a graduate student and funding from the Summerlee Foundation of Dallas, we began to collect information about forts, battlefields, and historic structures from the Gulf of Mexico to Laredo. We planned to create a web-based "virtual" trail with a paper map/trail guide, audio podcasts, and educational traveling trunks containing replicas of items typical of Civil War life in this region, such as uniforms, camp gear, currency, and coins as well as a formal set of lesson plans geared to statewide curriculum guidelines. In late 2013, we met with the cities of Roma and Rio Grande City and the Brownsville Community Improvement Corporation and secured additional funding, which allowed us to proceed and bring together a group of community and professional supporters from across the region and country to discuss the feasibility and support for the creation of a Civil War trail.

On May 22, 2014, less than one year before the sesquicentennial observations of the last battle of the American Civil War—at Palmito Ranch near Brownsville, Texas—we made our first effort toward building this trail. Suspecting that there was a great deal of information retained in the living memory of community members, a meeting was convened at which nearly fifty individuals representing a broad swath of the community came together. We requested that with guidance from three "Project Scholars" in Civil War history (Dr. Jerry Thompson, Texas A&M International Regents Professor; Dr. W. Stephen McBride, Director of Archaeology, Camp Nelson Civil War Heritage Park, Kentucky; and Dr. James Leiker, Director, Kansas Studies Institute), they comb their individual neighborhoods to tap into the region's lore. A mere seven months later, the English portion of the Rio Grande Valley Civil War Trail web page went live. Then, in February 2015, the Spanish narratives, English-language podcasts, and the bilingual map/brochure were complete. On February 28, 2015, a little more than nine months after the initial meeting, the trail was officially launched at a ribbon cutting ceremony held at the university.

Much has happened since that official opening. Drawing upon the historical materials that community members provided as well as original archival research by participating historical and archaeological professionals, two books are now completed and in the process of publication by the Texas A & M University Press. Funding from the Summerfield G. Roberts Foundation of Dallas has produced twenty traveling trunks—miniature portable museums containing items typical of Civil War life in this region—for distribution to local school districts; a set of 56 lesson plans that are aligned to objectives in the Social Studies Texas Essential Knowledge and Skills (TEKS) for both elementary and secondary schools with a primary focus on grades 4, 7, 8, and Advanced Placement (AP) US History; and now this book.

Which brings me back to why we produced this book. As noted above, this is a severely under told story about which we cannot expect anyone who has not been intimately connected with the overall project to have much background knowledge. In providing a general short overview of the Civil War Era here, we have two main audiences in mind. First, we intend this book as a frame of reference for teachers who might want to incorporate our lesson plans and artifacts into their teaching. As Dr. Rolando Avila has pointed out in the introduction to the lesson plan book, "curriculum with a focus on the local helps students develop stronger ties to their community and helps them become productive citizens," yet we realize that emphasis on the local has to be placed in the larger context of region, nation, and world. This book seeks to provide that context. The second audience we have in mind is people who are interested more generally in the history of this geographical area but who have had little or no formal introduction to what happened here during the Civil War. For them we hope this book, with its narrative and brief bibliography of further readings, might serve as an entry point for finding out more about that history. In order to reach both of those potential audiences, Dr. Avila has labored to keep the story straightforward, brief, and free from the jargon that too often makes academic writing inaccessible.

It is the hope of all of those who have contributed to the creation and growth of the Rio Grande Valley Civil War Trail project that readers will find this brief introduction both rewarding and entertaining. We also hope that this book will find its way to a broad audience which may come to appreciate this project and the vision of place-based education upon which it is based.

Christopher L. Miller
Professor, History
Associate Director, CHAPS Program
The University of Texas Rio Grande Valley

Chapter 1: On the Road to Civil War (1836-1860)

Republic of Texas (1836-1845)

By the 1830s, Texans had become dissatisfied with Mexican rule. With the Texas Revolution (1835-1836), Texans declared and won their independence from Mexico. Mexican General Santa Anna signed the two Treaties of Velasco, which ended the fighting, gave Santa Anna's promise that he would work for Mexican recognition of Texas Independence, and hinted that the border between Mexico and Texas would be the Rio Grande. However, the Mexican government refused to ratify either of the two treaties. Consequently, the site of the official boundary remained unresolved. The former southern Mexican boundary between Coahuila and Tejas had traditionally been the Nueces River (near Corpus Christi), but Texas now claimed all the land to the Rio Grande. The boundary dispute would remain unsettled for several years and would eventually become an important factor in bringing on a war between Mexico and the United States.

David G. Burnet served as a temporary president of Texas for about half a year while the new nation established its government. Like the US Constitution, the 1836 Texas Constitution divided political power into three branches. Also, the Texas Constitution contained a Bill of Rights that guaranteed Texas citizens certain rights including freedom of speech and freedom of religion. However, the Texas Constitution was much more explicit in its protection of the institution of slavery. According to Texas constitutional law, even African Americans who had fought for Texas independence were denied rights that were guaranteed to all white free men. Greenbury Logan, an African American Texas patriot, lamented being deprived of "every privilege dear to a freeman." According to Logan, free African American Texans had "no vote or say in any way."

Many Tejanos (Mexican Texans) also suffered hardships in the new nation. Most white Texans erroneously assumed that all Tejanos had opposed Texas independence. The misinformed perception fueled animosity. In addition, Texas had an abundance of land, which attracted about 7,000 settlers each year. Many of settlers took land from Tejanos by force. For example, fearing for their safety, the de Leon family of Victoria forfeited their land holdings when they fled from Texas. In January 1840, prominent Tejanos (including Jesús de Cárdenas, Antonio Canales Rosillo, Antonio Zapata, and José María Jesús Carbajal) held a convention in which they declared their independence from Mexico. They claimed land between Mexico and Texas (the areas of Tamaulipas and Coahuila north to the Nueces and Median rivers) to form the Republic of the Rio Grande (1840). The Tejano leaders established the new nation's capital in Laredo. However, in November of the same year, the Mexican army destroyed the republic.

On October 22, 1836, Sam Houston (former Commander-in-Chief of the Texas Army) was elected the second president of the Republic of Texas. In 1837, the US recognized Texas as a nation. Recognition from France, Great Britain, and the Netherlands followed a few years later. In 1839, leaders established the capital of the republic at Austin. That same year, the government adopted the Lone Star flag as the official flag of the new nation. In several ways, the new nation seemed to be off to a good start. However, Texas faced two major challenges: debt and the threat of attack. During the revolution, Texas leaders had borrowed money to pay for weapons. Consequently, Texas was faced with a tremendous debt, which threatened future national stability. Although Houston tried to find ways to alleviate the debt, there was little he could do. As immigrants settled in Texas, some Native American tribes (including the Comanche and the Kiowa) fought to defend their lands. The violence resulted in atrocities on both sides. In addition, some Mexican leaders refused to accept the independence of Texas and threatened to regain the northern Mexican territory. For this reason, some Texans feared a possible Mexican attack.

{Figure 01.01} Sam Houston

These fears were not without merit. In March of 1842 a Mexican army of about 500 men invaded Texas and occupied San Antonio, Goliad, and Refugio. General Rafael Vasquez raised the Mexican flag in San Antonio and declared that Texas was once again Mexican territory. Several days later, Vasquez and his army returned to Mexico, and in their absence Texans regained control of the land. In September of the same year, Mexican General Adrian Woll occupied San Antonio with an army of about 1,400 men. This time, the Texas militia and the Texas Rangers drove the Mexican army out of Texas. By the end of 1842, leaders could boast that they had kept Texas safe from permanent Mexican occupation. However, the Mexican government refused to recognize Texas as an independent nation. In fact, many Mexicans felt that Texas was merely Mexican territory that was temporarily in rebellion. In light of these challenges, Texas would have to either fend for itself or look to the US for help. Houston explained: "My great desire is that our country of Texas shall be annexed to the United States.... It is policy to hold out the idea that we are very able to sustain ourselves against any power..., yet I am free to say to you that we cannot do it."

State of Texas

Many Texans believed that the answer to the nation's challenges was to renounce nationhood in exchange for US statehood. Sam Houston was a notable supporter of annexation, and he tried to show others some advantages of his point of view. For example, Americans were confident that the well-equipped US military was able to protect them from invasion. In general terms, the US had an infrastructure that made it possible to deliver services (like the US mail) to its citizens. In contrast, Texas could not afford these kinds of benefits. However, not all Texans agreed with Houston's view. Some Texans wanted Texas to remain an independent nation that might one day grow to be powerful and wealthy. Some Americans also rejected the idea of annexation. American abolitionists did not want another slave holding state added to the Union. Other Americans did not like the idea of inheriting Texas's debt. In addition, the long standing unresolved boundary dispute between Mexico and Texas gained great significance in all annexation negotiations.

In spite of these objections, ultimately the fervor for westward expansion swayed the majority of public opinion in favor of annexation. The idea that the US should expand from the Atlantic to the Pacific Oceans had been a fixture in American thought since the establishment of the original thirteen colonies. Expansion was seen by many Americans as a right. Michigan Senator (and future candidate for president) Lewis Cass explained, "We do not want the people of Mexico either as citizens or as subjects. All we want is their land." An editorial in John L. O'Sullivan's *Democratic Review* (published in Washington D.C.) articulated the idea of the God given right of American westward expansion as "Manifest Destiny." During the presidential election of 1844, James K. Polk promised to fulfill Manifest Destiny. The popularity of Polk's platform won him the election and convinced the majority of the US Congress to support the annexation of Texas.

The annexation process took almost an entire year. On February 28, 1845, the US Congress passed a resolution that granted Texas the permission to become a state. Next, it was up to the Texas Congress and Texas voters to accept the offer. Before Texans could vote on the issue of annexation, Great Britain and France sent diplomats to Mexico to try to convince the Mexican government to offer Texas a deal; Mexico would be willing to recognize the independence of Texas only if Texas agreed to reject annexation. The Texas Congress rejected Mexico's proposal and instead passed the resolution for annexation on July 4, 1845 (with only one "no" vote). Texas voters accepted the resolution in October. Out of about 4,000 voters, only about 200 Texans voted against it. Annexation was made official on December 29, 1845. In a public ceremony in front of the state capital, Anson Jones (the last president of Texas) lowered the Texas flag and stated, "The final act of this great drama is now performed; the Republic of Texas is no more." Jones then raised the US flag. Texas became the 28th US state.

Mexican American War (1846-1848)

The annexation agreement between Texas and the US specified that the official southern boundary of the state of Texas was the Rio Grande. However, Mexico did not agree. Newly elected President Polk was eager to deliver on his promise to fulfill Manifest Destiny, and he believed that negotiations with Mexico would facilitate further acquisition of southwestern Mexican territory (including California). Polk sent John Slidell to Mexico City with orders to negotiate the Mexico-Texas boundary dispute. However, Mexican authorities refused to meet with Slidell. Polk then ordered General Zachary Taylor to lead his troops from New Orleans to Texas. Taylor arrived at the north side of the mouth of the Rio Grande in April 1846 and built Fort Texas (later renamed Fort Brown after Major Jacob Brown, its fallen commander).

Mexico stood firm in its view that the official Mexico-Texas southern border was at the Nueces River, and they viewed US military presence along the Rio Grande as an invasion of Mexican territory. On April 22, Mexico declared war against the US. In early May, Mexican and American troops fought north of the Rio Grande at the Battle of Palo Alto and then at the Battle of Resaca de la Palma. Concurrently, a large garrison of Mexican troops in Matamoros began shelling the fort, which stood adjacent to the river. The US Congress declared war on May 13, 1846. Soon after, Porfirio Diaz (future president of Mexico) uttered his famous statement: "Alas, poor Mexico, so far from God and so close to the United States." In his memoirs, US Grant reflected: "The Mexican War was one of the most unjust ever waged by a strong nation against a weaker nation."

{Figure 01.02} Porfirio Diaz

On December 22, 1847, Abraham Lincoln stood before Congress and delivered his "Spot Resolution" speech in opposition to the Mexican American War. Congressman Lincoln quoted Polk's message to Congress in which the president claimed that Mexico had invaded the state of Texas "shedding the blood of our citizens on our own soil." Lincoln then asked the president to identify the spot where the blood was shed. Lincoln's argument centered on the fact that it was common knowledge that the territory in which the battles occurred was, in fact, disputed territory. The main reason that Lincoln and the Whig Party opposed the war was that they believed US victory would result in the addition of slave-holding territory to the nation. In spite of the Lincoln's opposition, the war went on. Lincoln's prediction came true, and the addition of huge amounts of slave territory to the nation increased the existing tensions between slave and anti-slave factions.

Palo Alto Battlefield

The prairie of Palo Alto and the nearby field Resaca de la Palma were scenes of a battle from the U.S-Mexican War, but the sites also had significance to the Civil War. Dozens of young officers who experienced some of their first combat in the clashes with Mexican troops on May 8th and 9th 1846, moved up to positions of leadership in the Civil War. Ulysses S. Grant, George Gordon Meade, Don Carlos Buell, and 21 others became Generals in the Union army. James Longstreet, John Pemberton and 12 more of their peers became Generals in the Confederate ranks. Edmund Kirby Smith who was a lieutenant at Palo Alto, commanded the Trans-Mississippi Department of the Confederacy, which included Texas and the Rio Grande Valley.

Excerpt from UTRGV Civil War Trail – University of Texas Rio Grande Valley

Years later, historians identified the Mexican cession as a major long-term cause of the American Civil War. Many US troops who fought alongside each other during the Mexican American War (including U.S. Grant, George Meade, and James Longstreet) found themselves on opposite sides during the Civil War about a decade later.

The Mexican American War ended in 1848 with the signing of the Treaty of Guadalupe Hidalgo, which ceded nearly one-third of Mexico's territory to the US (including present-day California, Nevada, and Utah and parts of Arizona, New Mexico, Colorado, and Wyoming). In fact, during Polk's presidency (1845-1849), more than one million square miles of

{Figure 01.03} Congressman Abraham Lincoln

new territory were added to the nation. Other terms of the treaty included that the US would pay Mexico $15 million and agree to allow Mexicans living on the land to remain if they chose to do so. Another term of the treaty, that was to have a significant impact on the Rio Grande Valley, designated the Rio Grande an international waterway "free and common to the vessels and citizens of both countries." A major accomplishment of the treaty was that it finally settled the Texas question as well as the boundary dispute by setting the Mexico-Texas southern border along the Rio Grande. To secure the recognized border, the US built forts along the river. Besides Fort Brown (Brownsville), the US also built Fort Ringgold (Rio Grande City), and Fort McIntosh (Laredo).

{Figure 01.04} Juan Nepomuceno Cortina in 1865

Growth and the "First Cortina War"

In 1848, the boundaries of Texas were unclear. Some felt they extended into much of present-day New Mexico and parts of Oklahoma, Kansas, Colorado, and Wyoming. Boundary disputes arose in Coahuila, Tamaulipas, and New Mexico. The present-day northwestern boundary of Texas came about due to a Congressional compromise. New Mexico residents pushed for the change, because they wanted to be an independent territory. Henry Clay included a solution to this northwestern Texas territory dispute in the Compromise of 1850. According to the compromise, Texas gave up its claims to the disputed land. In exchange, the US government gave Texas $10 million for the forfeited land. The funds made it possible for Texas to get out of debt. Texas also used some of the money to create a permanent fund for the state public school system. Texas built school buildings, a new state capital, a governor's mansion, and a hospital. Farming, ranching, and various kinds of free enterprise ventures sprung up.

Jackson Ranch

Along the Rio Grande in Hidalgo County lay the Jackson Ranch and Eli Jackson Cemetery, once owned by Nathaniel Jackson, a loyal Unionist during the Civil War. In the 1850's, Jackson left Alabama with his African-American wife Matilda Hicks, his son Eli, and other adult children. They hoped to escape the intolerance of inter-racial marriage they had known in the South. Accompanying the Jacksons were eleven African-American freedmen. In 1857, Jackson founded his ranch on a former Spanish grant. His property is said to have become a refuge for runaway slaves from Texas and the Deep South. Today, many people know about the Underground Railroad that shepherded enslaved people to freedom in the northern states and Canada, but few know about the route to freedom in Mexico.

Excerpt from UTRGV Civil War Trail – University of Texas Rio Grande Valley

In like manner, the lower Rio Grande Valley enjoyed a period of economic stability after the Mexican American War. Veterans of the Mexican American War (including capitalists like Richard King and Mifflin Kenedy) settled in the area. Other settlers (including Charles Stillman, John Vale, John McAllen, and John Young) became wealthy merchants, traders, and ranch owners. The lower Rio Grande Valley seemed like an attractive refuge where mixed race families (including the Webbers, Jacksons, Brewsters, Rutledges, and Singleterrys) settled to get away from the cruelties of racism in the American South.

The old Spanish families that lived in the region held legal claim to their land through Spanish land grants. By 1850, envious settlers attempted to annul all land titles in the region. Lawsuits ruined some local landowners. In the late 1850s, María Estéfana Goseascochea de Cortina was forced to sell thousands of acres of land to pay her attorneys to defend her

{Figure 01.05} Captain Richard King

First Cortina War

Juan Cortina was born to a cattle-ranching family in the state of Tamaulipas, Mexico in 1824. When he was still young, Cortina's mother inherited portions of a large land grant in the lower Rio Grande valley, including the area that surrounded Brownsville, to which the family relocated. Like many of his contemporaries, Cortina objected to the unfair treatment that landowners of Mexican descent received in Texas following the Treaty of Guadalupe Hidalgo in 1848, leading in 1859 to a series of violent confrontations collectively called the "First Cortina War." In late September, after having shot local marshal Robert Shears, Cortina led a party of armed men who seized the town of Brownsville. A counter posse called the "Brownsville Tigers" formed to oppose Cortina's force and he abandoned the town, fleeing to the family ranch. There, in November, Cortina easily routed the attacking Brownsville Tigers. Soon after, a company of Texas Rangers attempted to take Cortina, but he defeated them as well.

In the following month, a second group of Rangers led by Captain John "Rip" Ford arrived and joined with US forces at Fort Brown. Cortina retreated up the Rio Grande. On December 27, 1859, the combined army and ranger force engaged him in the Battle of Rio Grande City. Cortina's forces were decisively defeated and Cortina fled into Mexico. In one final blow against his enemies, Cortina attempted to capture the steamboat *Ranchero*, owned and operated by two of his antagonists, Richard King and Mifflin Kenedy, only to be defeated again on February 4, 1860 in the Battle of La Bolsa. He then remained in Mexico, only to return when the Civil War opened new opportunities to pursue old grievances. It was as a result of Cortina's activities that Colonel Robert E. Lee (USA) visited Ringgold Barracks in 1860.

Excerpt from UTRGV Civil War Trail – University of Texas Rio Grande Valley

land ownership claims. Juan Nepomuceno Cortina, one of her sons, claimed that the family land had been lost due to fraud. Cortina's discontent led to the "First Cortina War" in the summer and fall of 1859. Cortina's guerilla army of about 600 men clashed with the Texas militia and the Texas Rangers until December 1859 when a combined force of Rangers and US

Army regulars drove Cortina into Mexico. From the Mexican side of the Rio Grande, Cortina attempted to capture the merchant steamboat *Ranchero* (owned by Richard King and Mifflin Kenedy). However, Cortina was defeated at the Battle of La Bolsa on February 4, 1860. As a result of Cortina's attacks, Colonel Robert E. Lee visited Ringgold Barracks in 1860. Lee conducted his investigation at the commandant's quarters, which were later preserved and named the "Robert E. Lee House."

1860 US Presidential Election

In the two decades preceding the Civil War, the population in the North had exploded. Massive waves of immigrants

{Figure 01.06} Wooden structures of Ringgold Barracks along the Rio Grande

came from Europe to work in Northern factories. Each immigrant, whether or not he voted, was counted toward representation, but, because of the Three-Fifths Compromise in the United State Constitution, slaves were only counted as three-fifths of a person. The Electoral College was based on population, and as a consequence, the North had a tremendous edge over the South in the 1860 presidential election. Lincoln's nomination by the Republican Party on May 9, 1860, increased the already existing sectional tensions between the North and the South. The *Boston Herald*, a Democratic Newspaper, reported that "the nomination in many respects [was] a strong one, and [would] be difficult to defeat." New Yorker George Tempelton Strong recorded in his diary that, by this point, "Lincoln's election seem[ed] to be conceded."

Region	Total Population	Total Population Counted Toward Representation
South	9,038,910	7,792,280
North	13,950,163	13,950,163
Source: 1850 US Census		

Region	US Representatives	US Senators
South	90	30
North	141	32
Source: Carol Berkin, Christopher L. Miller, Robert W. Cherny, and James L. Gormly. (2015). *Making America: A History of the United States*. 7th edition. Stanford, Connecticut: Cengage Learning, page 316.		

In November, 1860, Lincoln did not receive any Southern popular or electoral votes. Not a single person voted for Lincoln in Alabama, Georgia, Florida, Louisiana, Mississippi, South Carolina, Texas, Arkansas, Tennessee, or North Carolina. In fact, Lincoln did not even appear on the ballot in any of these ten states. In the midst of this opposition, Lincoln still arose victorious and became America's sixteenth president. Consequently, many Southerners did not recognize Lincoln as their president. Instead, they saw Lincoln as a leader who had been elected by the North and for the North.

{Figure 01.07} Abraham Lincoln c. 1861

Compromise, which had been a cornerstone in the history of American government, no longer seemed possible. Southerners were alarmed at the election results, because they were concerned that Republicans would pass anti-slavery laws that the South would be politically powerless to stop. How could they allow the North to take their slave property? They believed that abolition of slavery would lead to ruin in the South.

Chapter 2: Early Civil War Years (1861-1862)

Secession and the Start of the Civil War

Following the presidential election, debates about secession ensued in Southern state legislatures, and most of the slave states voted to seceded from the Union. Before Lincoln was elected in November 1860, there were thirty-three states in the Union. By the time of Lincoln's inauguration in March of 1861, there were twenty-seven states left. In the months following his inauguration, four more states seceded.

Southern leaders sought to set up their own government in which they could have a voice and better representation of their interests, values, and culture. The editor of the *Alexandria Sentinel* wrote, "We of the South have thus imposed upon us a government outside of ourselves, and founded on a sentiment hostile to our social system." The *Baltimore Daily Republican* assessed, "Abraham Lincoln has been voted for and by the North...but it is very doubtful...he will ever be President of the *United* States."

Lincoln would not allow, or even recognize, secession. In spite of the South's motivation to secede, Lincoln also had a very strong political motivation to stop the South from seceding. Lincoln recognized that if the South was allowed to secede, it would set a dangerous precedent that would threaten the future of the North itself. Not only would the North be more vulnerable to outside attack, but it would also be unable to stop any more Northern states from seceding in the future. In Lincoln's view, if the South were allowed to secede, it would inevitably lead to the complete political destruction of the rest of the Nation.

Texas was slow to secede mostly due to Texas Governor Sam Houston's loyalty to the Union. Houston explained to his fellow Texans:

> All you know that I am opposed to secession, and all of you know my convictions on the subject. I have taken an oath to support the Constitution of the United States and its flag and the Constitution of Texas and its flag.... Gentlemen, you cannot forget those two flags—you cannot withdraw from the Union.

Over Houston's objection, a group of Texas leaders (including Texas Supreme Court Chief Justice John Salmon "Rip" Ford) organized a state convention, which met on January 28, 1861. On February 1, the convention passed a secession ordinance by a vote of 166 to 8, which repealed the 1845 annexation agreement with the US. Houston had attempted to undermine the convention by asking the Texas Legislature to declare it illegal. However, the majority of the legislature supported the convention's plan. After the convention's vote, Houston insisted that the people of Texas be given an opportunity to either accept or reject secession. The convention members agreed to a popular referendum and scheduled it for February 23.

In the weeks leading up to the vote, national and state events made the idea of secession more attractive to many Texans. For example, the Confederate States of America (CSA) adopted a constitution (February 8), Jefferson Davis was elected CSA President (February 9), and Union Brigadier General David E. Twiggs surrendered federal forts in Texas (February 16). In truth, even before these events, most Texans supported secession. This trend also applied to most people in the lower Rio Grande Valley. There was, however, one glaring exception. In Zapata County, many voters preferred to stay in the Union.

Texas voters approved secession by a vote of 46,129 to 14,697 making Texas the 7th state to secede from the Union. Within a few days, the convention passed an ordinance uniting Texas with the CSA. When the convention ordered all state officials to take an oath of allegiance to the CSA, Houston

{Figure 02.01} John Salmon "Rip" Ford

refused. Consequently, the convention removed Houston from office and replaced him with a new governor. When Lincoln (who had been inaugurated US President on March 4) heard of Houston's loyalty, he offered to send federal troops to Texas to keep him in office. Although Houston disagreed with the direction that Texas had chosen, he respected the will of the people. Houston declined Lincoln's offer and explained to his Texas supporters:

> Would you be willing to deluge the capital of Texas with the blood of Texans, merely to keep one poor old man in a position for a few more days longer, in a position that belongs to the people? No! Go tell my deluded friends that I am proud of their friendship, of their love and loyalty,...[but] to go to their homes and to conceal from the world that they would have been guilty of such an act.

On April 12, Confederates fired on Fort Sumter (South Carolina) and ignited the Civil War across the nation. More than 60,000 Texans served in the war. Some Texans fought for the Union, but most of them fought for the Confederacy.

Texas leaders set up mustering stations as well as training camps. The most popular branch of service was the cavalry. A British observer reported, "...no Texan walks a yard if he can help it...." Camp Bosque near Waco and Camp Clark on the San Marcos River trained recruits with drills in marching and using weapons. Some camps also included Olympic-type activities such as running, jumping, boxing, and wresting competitions. It was not surprising, therefore, that soldiers would sometimes engage in these types of activities to overcome boredom after weeks of inactivity in the field. With four out of five white military age men in the war, Texas women managed homes, farms, and plantations. Some women became teachers, which had been exclusively a male occupation. Some women volunteered in hospitals while others made bandages. A handful of women (including Sarah Edmonds Seelye, Jennie Hodgers, and Frances Clayton) served in the army disguised as men.

In the Rio Grande Valley, a controversy over the popular referendum sparked a revolt that began the fighting of the Civil

War in the region. In an attempt to squash the pro-Union sentiment in Zapata County, County Judge Isidro Vela announced that anyone who failed to vote in favor of secession would be fined. Although the vote to join the Confederacy was reported as unanimous (212 to 0) by county officials, there were several prominent citizens who demanded that Zapata County remain within the Union. An influential resident, Antonio Ochoa, rallied several Union supporters and confronted Judge Vela in April 1861 at Carrizo, the county seat for Zapata County. After a long meeting, Vela persuaded Ochoa and his supporters to return peacefully to their homes.

Second Cortina War

With the outbreak of Civil War in both the United States and Mexico, the notorious Juan Nepomuceno Cortina returned to the north bank of the Rio Grande. In May 1861, he splashed across the river with about thirty of his Cortinistas and sacked Carrizo, the county seat of Zapata County. In a forty-minute fight, however, Confederate Captain Santos Benavides decisively defeated Cortina, killing or capturing several of his men and driving what remained across the river into Mexico.

Excerpt from UTRGV Civil War Trail – University of Texas Rio Grande Valley

---

Several days after the confrontation, a Confederate Cavalry unit commanded by Captain (later Colonel) Santos Benavides, stationed in Laredo, arrived in Carrizo. Following Benavides' arrival, Vela ordered Ochoa's arrest. Benavides and his unit proceeded to El Clareño where Ochoa and his supporters lived. A battle ensued in which numerous civilians were killed. The news of the massacre spread quickly throughout Zapata County and other communities on both sides of the border.

The deaths at El Clareño resulted in stronger local opposition to the Confederacy. When the news reached Cortina, he joined the fight against the Confederacy in what came to be called the "Second Cortina War." On May 21, 1861, Cortina and his troops surrounded Benavides and his unit at Redmond's Ranch. However, Confederate reinforcements soon arrived from Laredo, causing Cortina to retreat across the Rio Grande.

Ford's 1861 Rio Grande Mission

Two months before Confederates fired on Fort Sumter, John S. "Rip" Ford was commissioned colonel of cavalry and sent to the Rio Grande with orders to take over federal forts along the river. Ford arrived at Brazos Santiago in late February and found a caretaker crew on duty including Lieutenant James Thompson (the commander) and twelve artillerymen. Within a few hours, Ford convinced Thompson to surrender the fort. After Ford and Thompson conducted a short ceremony in which they lowered the US flag and raised the Lone Star flag, the federal troops departed peacefully.

The next day, Ford went to Brownsville and met with Captain Bennett H. Hill, the commander at Fort Brown. Unlike Thompson, Hill was unwilling to leave his post without orders from his superiors. Even after news that Twiggs had forfeited federal forts in Texas had reached Brownsville, Hill remained determined to defend his position if necessary. After more than a week of unfruitful negotiations, the standoff ended on March 3 when US Major Fitzjohn Porter ordered the evacuation of federal troops at Fort Brown by way of the *Daniel Webster* steamer.

Consequently, Ford secured Brazos Santiago and Fort Brown without firing a shot. His job was now to reinforce his position against possible attacks from Native Americans, Mexicans, and US troops. He decided to abandon Brazos Santiago for three main reasons: It had no access to fresh water, its sand earthworks provided weak defense, and, most importantly, its guns had limited range; an enemy warship could bombard

Brazos Santiago from a position beyond the range of the island's guns. Ford and his troops were busy building up Fort Brown's defenses when news of the fall of Fort Sumter reached them.

After both Lincoln and Davis called for volunteers to fight the Civil War, preparations at Fort Brown became more urgent. Ford asked the Brownsville mayor for help. Brownsville citizens dug trenches. Local merchants volunteered supplies and helped move guns and equipment from Brazos Santiago to Fort Brown with the use of steamboats and mule teams. In late

{Figure 02.02} Confederate Colonel John Salmon "Rip" Ford

April 1861, Ford reported to his superiors that Fort Brown was ready. Colonel McCulloch ordered Ford out of the Rio Grande Valley in April 1862, but Fort Brown remained under Confederate control and guarded by 400 men. In fact, there were 1,200 Confederate troops stationed between the mouth of the Rio Grande and Ringgold Barracks at Rio Grande City.

Shortages

Since most US factories were in the North, when the Confederacy seceded from the Union, it experienced immediate shortages in both military and domestic products. In 1861, many volunteers to the Confederate military furnished their own weapons (including hunting rifles, muskets, and shot guns). In fact, some Texans used lances throughout the war. As Texas troops took over federal forts, more weapons and ammunition became available to them. Additionally, Texas had several factories that were exclusively dedicated to making weapons for the Confederacy. One of the largest factories of this type was located in Tyler. Other larger factories were in Austin, Dallas, and Galveston. In spite of this, the Confederacy was unable to meet weapons demands, and it relied heavily on imports.

Since priority was given to the war effort, the home front suffered from a scarcity of all products including bread, pins and needles, salt, medicine, clothing, shoes, paper, farm implements, and coffee. The Confederacy suffered from bread riots in Mobile, Atlanta, and Richmond. In the absence of needed products, Texans devised substitutes. For example, some women used mesquite thorns as needle and pin substitutes. Some Confederate newspapers went out of print, because of the paper shortage. Other newspapers adopted a smaller size. Several recipes for coffee substitutes existed. One mixture required peanuts, potatoes, beans, and peas. One Texan assessed the concoction as a "wretched imitation, though gulped down, when chilly and tired, for lack of anything better."

Anaconda Plan

On June 29, 1861, Lincoln called several generals to a meeting to discuss the state of the Union. General Winfield Scott (a veteran of the War of 1812 and the Mexican American War) proposed a blockade of Southern ports as a way of starving the South into submission. Lincoln believed Scott (the "Grand Old Man of the Army") to be his most experienced and strategically qualified general. Even after the Confederacy had demonstrated its aggressive stance at Fort Sumter, Lincoln pursued a policy of moderation. The Anaconda Plan, suggested by Scott, was a prime example of this kind of limited war strategy. The blockade of Southern ports was intended to isolate the South both economically and diplomatically from Europe. Slowly but surely, the blockade would choke trade and the South's economy would suffer. In addition, a bad economy would limit the South's ability to wage war. This economic hardship brought on by isolation, Lincoln believed, would encourage a voluntary return to the Union.

When the plan was executed in early July, the North only had forty-two commissioned warships in its entire Navy, which were scattered all over the globe. Of that number, only twenty-six were steamers. The rest were sailing ships. Even after most of them were ordered to take their positions near Confederate ports, they were ill prepared to effectively patrol the 3,500 miles of Southern coastline. However, even though the Anaconda Plan got off to a weak start, the Union Navy was able to increase its grip on the Confederate coastline each year. According to historical Frank L. Owsley, the ratio of safe arrivals of blockade runners to those captured was nine to one in 1861; seven to one in 1862; four to one in 1863; three to one in 1864, and one to one in 1865. Although the Confederacy was low on hard currency, it had an abundance of cotton. If it could trade cotton for needed products, it could wage war. By 1862, wagons carrying cotton from Arkansas, Louisiana, and East Texas made their way to the Rio Grande. Trade with foreign nations alleviated certain shortages, but it did not eradicate them.

In Texas, blockade runners visited several ports including Corpus Christi. However, Galveston (the largest Texas port city) was their favorite destination. On July 2, 1861, the US Navy initiated a blockade of Galveston. As the US Navy continually strengthened blockade efforts, Confederates began to rely more heavily on trade through the Rio Grande. The Treaty of Guadalupe Hidalgo designated the Rio Grande an international waterway. Consequently, the US was prevented by its own treaty with Mexico from blockading the Rio Grande. Historian James A. Irby explained, "This unpretentious, muddy river came to serve as the funnel through which the contraband from Europe and the West Indies passed into the Confederacy."

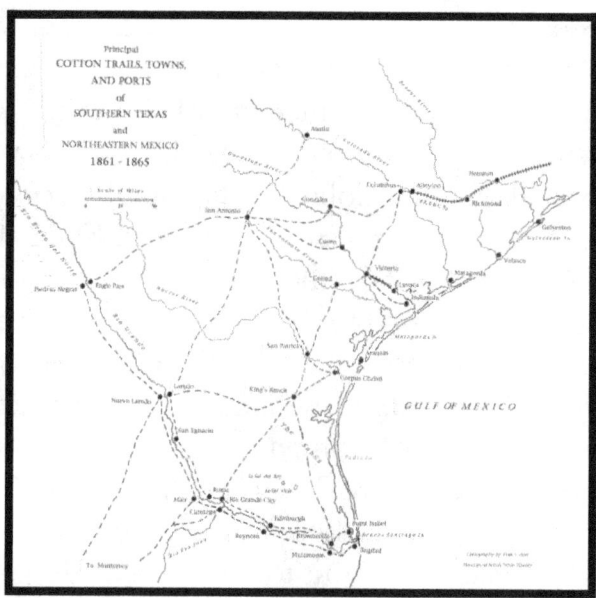

{Figure 02.03} Cotton Trails sketch by Tom A. Fort

Mexico: European Invasion and Civil War

With the Monroe Doctrine (1823), the US barred European nations from creating any new American colonies. However, during the chaos of the American Civil War, US enforcement of the Monroe Doctrine was not a priority. Consequently, Europeans saw a window of opportunity. Spain invaded Mexico in December 1861. British and French troops joined the invasion force a couple of weeks later. The Spanish and British justified their temporary occupation of Mexico as a means to collect unpaid debts. On the other hand, French monarch Napoleon III had a much more ambitious goal: the permanent colonization of Mexico under French rule.

Civil War between Conservatives and Liberals had dominated Mexico for decades before the European invasion. Conservatives believed that leadership of government should be restricted to an educated few. Conservatives sought to limit suffrage, civil liberties, and social services. In contrast, Liberals advocated universal male suffrage, wide civil liberties, religious freedom, and a decentralized national government. Liberals had been victorious in the past two civil wars. However, Conservatives saw the invasion as an opportunity to reverse their past failures.

{Figure 02.04} Benito Juarez/Emperor Maximilian

> **Benito Juarez**
>
> For many Mexican citizens, Benito Juarez remains the most highly regarded of presidents and to this day is the only Mexican president honored with the title of Benémerito de las Americas (Hero of the Americas). Born 1806 to Zapotec Indians, he received a basic seminary education and later graduated with a law degree from the Oaxacan Institute of Sciences and Arts. Juarez became known as an educator, lawyer, and member of the Oaxacan state legislature. After being elected to the national Chamber of Deputies, he emerged as a prominent Liberal leader, helping to draft the Constitution of 1857 that extended rights to Mexican people. One provision of that charter, known as the Ley Juarez, abolished the legal privileges of the Church and the military.
>
> When Conservatives initiated a civil war aimed at annulling this constitution, Juarez led the Liberal forces to victory in the ensuing War of the Reform (1857-1860). When the subsequent French invasion reached Mexico City, he refused to surrender and instead retreated to the north of México. Juarez and Abraham Lincoln shared much in common, sympathizing with each other's cause during the civil wars faced by their respective nations. After the defeat of the French and the execution of Maximilian, Juarez resumed his duties as president in 1867. He was reelected to that post and served until his death in 1872.
>
> *Excerpt from UTRGV Civil War Trail – University of Texas Rio Grande Valley*

The Spanish and British evacuated their troops from Mexico on April 19, 1862, but the French remained intent on conquest. On May 5, 1862 (*Cinco de Mayo*), Mexican troops repelled the French at the Battle of Puebla. One year later, however, the French captured Mexico City. On April 10, 1864, Ferdinand Maximilian Joseph von Habsburg was crowned emperor of Mexico by a group of Conservatives. Liberals did not recognize Maximilian as the true ruler of Mexico. Instead, they supported Benito Juarez (the leader of the Liberal faction) who had been in power since 1857. Civil War (1862-1867) broke out between the Conservatives and the Liberals. Juarez and his followers set up base in the northern part of Mexico along the Rio

Grande. From there, Juarez secured needed weapons and supplies.

Rio Grande in 1862

According to historian James A. Irby, "A history of the Rio Grande Valley in the years 1861-1865 is largely a recounting of the struggle to control the region and the trade in cotton." By 1862, two civil wars were raging on both sides of the Rio Grande; one in the US and another in Mexico, and the ports of Matamoros and Bagdad supplied both wars.

In 1862, Union troops attacked Texas ports. In August, Union troops bombarded Corpus Christi, but could not capture the city. In October, the US Navy captured Galveston, and held on to the port city until Confederates wrestled it back on January 1, 1863. In December, Union troops captured Port Lavaca. During the same month, two Texas regiments serving in the Union marched along the river toward Rio Grande City and temporarily occupied Ringgold Barracks. But, the Union had its hands tied when it came to stopping the flow of goods through the Rio Grande; the "Backdoor of the Confederacy."

Rio Grande commerce was big business, and by 1862 communities along the river resembled the 1849 California gold rush boom towns. The cotton trade attracted a variety of people from all over the world (including gamblers, swindlers, and smugglers) to the region hoping to cash in. King, Kenedy, and Stillman, a local firm, made a fortune by securing government contracts to transport cotton on the river. King and Kenedy were influential businessmen who had built a ranching empire in the 1850s north of the lower Rio Grande Valley. Stillman was the founder of Brownsville and a target of Cortina's rage in 1859.

Eyewitnesses reported that the vessels anchored near Bagdad numbered 20 in September 1862, 60 to 70 in March 1863, and 200 to 300 in late 1864. In 1862, Commander Samuel

Swartwout of *USS Portmouth* was assigned to patrol the blockade near Brownsville. During that time, he witnessed ships transporting weapons, medicines, and other products to Mexico. But once in Mexico (and out of Swartwout's jurisdiction), many of the items were shipped to Texas across the Rio Grande. Likewise, ship's captains carrying Confederate cotton, if searched, would readily show false records indicating that the cargo was from Mexico. Swartwout reported to his superiors that he felt "satisfied it is impossible to prevent illicit trade on the Rio Grande unless we can take possession of…the American side of the Rio Grande…."

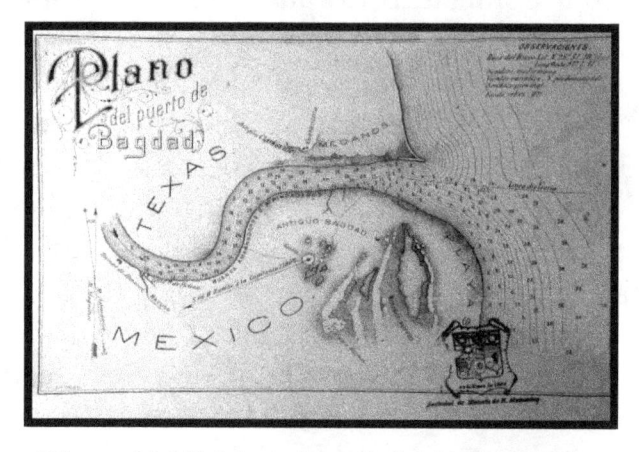

{Figure 02.05} Map of Bagdad, Mexico 1826

{Figure 02.06} Engraving of bustling Bagdad, Mexico, 1864-1865

{Figure 02.07} Engraving, Cotton bales on the Rio Grande

Rio Grande

It is not surprising that the Rio Grande itself played a central role in the history of the Civil War in the Rio Grande Valley. As Federal blockades sealed off the Confederate coastline, Mexico became a vital outlet for southerners to export their cotton. But the river's significance dates back much earlier. In the 1848 Treaty of Guadalupe Hidalgo, the United States and Mexico agreed that the waterway which divided their two nations would be an international river, open to merchants of both countries. In the 1860s, this agreement prohibited the Union Navy from halting shipments along the river. Merchants brought their cotton to Matamoros, loaded it on Mexican-registered steamboats, and transported it to Bagdad where it was transferred to larger ships for international distribution. Union forces could not halt this flow of supplies without widening the war's scope to Mexico, which was itself beset at that time by civil war. Although the US Army did briefly occupy towns of the Rio Grande Valley and slowed the flow of cotton southward, boats filled with cotton continued to ply the river's waters, unimpeded for the duration of the war.

Excerpt from UTRGV Civil War Trail – University of Texas Rio Grande Valley

After reading Swartwout's report, US Consul in Matamoros Leonard Pierce, Jr. added his views:

> I am afraid our Government undervalues the possession of this frontier. It is now grand thoroughfare for their foreign mails, passengers, commissioners, cotton, or, indeed, anything that they

wish. Of course, all the cotton that is shipped from this port comes from Texas, and it is probable that most of the merchandise brought here finds its way into the interior of the Southern states, and were this line occupied by our armies it would be giving a heavy blow to the rebellion.

Eventually, Lincoln heeded the advice and sent General Nathaniel Banks with orders to take control of Brownsville and shut down trade along the mouth of the Rio Grande. According to historian Ralph A. Wooster, "By the time of the Union occupation of Brownsville more than 150,000 bales of cotton had pass through Matamoros."

Chapter 3: Late Civil War Years (1863-1865)

Union Occupation and Confederate Response

On November 2, 1863, General Banks arrived at Brazos Island with a force of 7,000 men, which included members of the USCT. According to historian Jack D. Foner, 186,000 African Americans served in the Civil War and another 30,000 served in the Navy. Confederate General Hamilton P. Bee recognized that his troops were greatly outnumbered, and he ordered his men to evacuate Fort Brown and Brownsville. Bee also ordered the destruction of all military supplies and cotton that his men could not carry away with them. Consequently, when Banks arrived in Brownsville on the morning of November 6, 1863, he was unopposed. Instead of engaging Confederates, his men worked on putting out a large city fire, which had started when Bee burned his supplies.

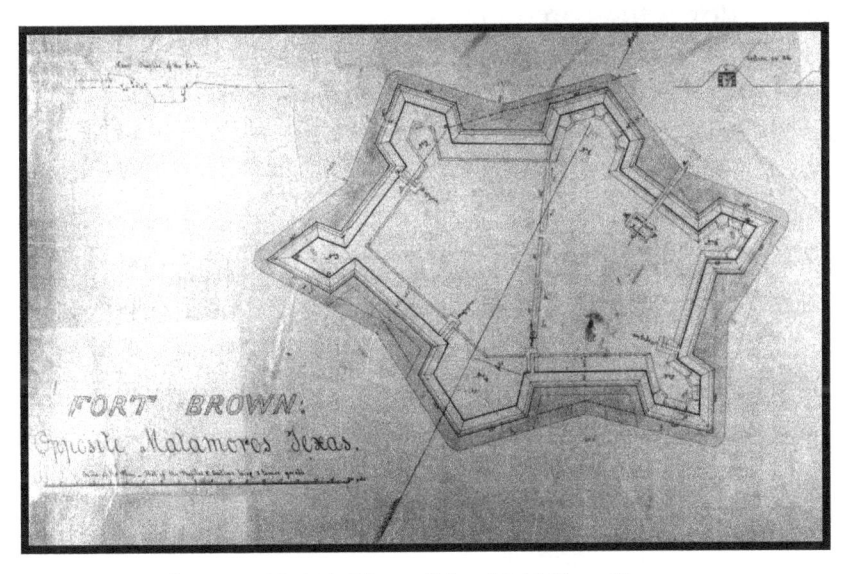

{Figure 03.01} Plan of the 1846 Fort Brown

With the Union in control of the US side of the Rio Grande at Brownsville, Confederates moved the cotton trade routes further north to Rio Grande City and Roma. Wishing to counter the Confederate trade shift, Banks captured Fort Ringgold in Rio Grande City. In response, Confederates found another way to circumvent Union troops. They moved the trade routes even further north to Laredo and Eagle Pass. By this time, Laredo was the major port of entry for Confederate cotton into Mexico. From Laredo, Confederates shipped cotton to the Mexican side of the river where it was then transported through Mexico to Matamoros and Bagdad. According to historian Ralph A. Wooster, "By the end of the war, 320,000 bales of cotton had been shipped across the Rio Grande."

Battle for Laredo

On March 19, 1864, Banks sent 200 men (the 2nd Texas Union Calvary) to Laredo with orders to seize cotton stores and shut down the Laredo trade. A Confederate scout informed Colonel Santos Benavides (the highest-ranking Tejano to serve the Confederacy) that 1,000 Union troops were on their way to Laredo. Benavides could not understand how such a large army could have gotten past his other scouts, but he immediately made plans to defend Laredo. Based on the only report he had, he believed that his men would be greatly outnumbered (by more than 10 to 1) in the coming battle.

Benavides had been very active during the war; in 1863, he had been authorized to raise his own force, which became known as Benavides's Regiment. For years, he had been in the field constantly without a tent or bed and often without blankets, without food, without water, and almost all the time riding through the country.

Colonel Santos Benavides

Colonel Santos Benavides became the highest-ranking Tejano to serve the Confederacy. Born in Laredo in 1823, he was a descendant of Tomás Sánchez de la Barrera y Garza, the founder of the small community. As a political and military leader in Laredo, Benavides brought a traditionally isolated region closer to the mainstream of Texas politics while preserving a sense of local independence. Assigned to the Rio Grande Military District at the beginning of the war, Benavides drove his rival Juan Cortina into Mexico at the battle of Carrizo in May 1861. He crushed other local revolts against Confederate authority on the Rio Grande. In November 1863 Benavides was authorized to raise his own force that became known simply as Benavides' Regiment. Perhaps his greatest triumph came on March 19, 1864 when he drove back more than two hundred soldiers from the Texas Union Cavalry. Benavides helped make possible the safe passage of cotton across the Rio Grande to Mexico during the Union occupation of the Lower Rio Grande Valley in 1863-64. During Reconstruction, Benavides remained active in his mercantile and ranching activities along with his brother Cristobal. He served three times in the Texas House of Representatives from 1879 to 1884, the only Tejano in the legislature at time, and twice served as alderman in Laredo. He died at his home in Laredo in 1891.

Excerpt from UTRGV Civil War Trail – University of Texas Rio Grande Valley

His years of service under hard conditions had taken a toll on his health. He had fallen ill from exhaustion, but he rose from his sick bed to address his men:

> This would not have happened had I not been confined to bed for some days. I would have known all about their advance and would have gone below and attacked them. As it is I have to fight to the last; though hardly able to stand I shall die fighting. I won't retreat, no matter what force the Yankees have—I know I can depend on my boys.

St. Augustine Plaza, Laredo

During the Civil War, St. Augustine's was a beehive of activity after Confederate officer Col. Santos Benavides established his headquarters here. Most Confederate troops were garrisoned in buildings on or near the plaza for much of the war. Laredo became particularly important when cotton moved across the river, especially after the federal occupation of the Lower Rio Grande Valley in late 1863 and early 1864. For the citizens of Laredo these were the "cotton times." Union forces attempted to destroy five thousand bales of cotton stacked in the plaza when they attacked the town in March 1864. Benavides and his men barricaded the streets with cotton bales and placed snipers on the buildings around the plaza.

Excerpt from UTRGV Civil War Trail –University of Texas Rio Grande Valley

By 1864, Benavides and the Confederate Tejano population he represented *were* the Confederacy on the Rio Grande. Benavides gave specific orders to his half-brother and chief aide Captain Cristobal Benavides:

> There are five thousand bales of cotton in…[San Augustin] [P]laza. It belongs to the Confederacy. If the day goes against us, fire it. Be sure to do the work properly so that not a bale of it shall fall into the hands of the Yankees. Then you will set my new house on fire, so that nothing of mine shall pass to the enemy. Let their victory be a barren one.

Benavides had a total of seventy-two men. He chose to lead forty-two of them to the outskirts of Laredo to try to stop the Union troops before they reached the town. He ordered the rest of the men to remain in town as a final defense.

{Figure 03.02} Colonel Santos Benavides

    The entire way, he was so ill that it was difficult for him to stay on his horse. He found a large corral that he thought would be a good place for his men to position themselves.

The corral provided his troops some cover and a clear field of fire on the advancing Union troops. No new scouting reports had reached him, so he still had no way of knowing the true number of Union troops that would attack, but he remained determined to defend his hometown at all cost.

Along Zacate Creek, the Union troops spotted the Benavides Regiment. Half a mile away from the corral, the Union troops dismounted their horses and formed groups of forty. After one group charged, a three-hour battle began. An eyewitness reported, "Benavides and his men fought with the coolest bravery." After three hours of fighting, the Union troops retreated. Benavides's Regiment did not suffer a single casualty. The next day, some of Benavides' troops searched for Union troops, but all they found were a few bloody trails in the sand, some blood-soaked rags, and five horses branded, "US" suggesting severe Union casualties.

{Figure 03.03} Zacate Creek view from south to north

Three days after the Battle for Laredo, a report of another impending Union attack reached Benavides. Although he was still ill, he mounted his horse and galloped out in front of his men ready to fight. However, even though he was willing to fight, his body was not able to do it. He was so weak that he fell from his horse and hit his head. After the accident, Benavides found out that the report was wrong. There was no immediate danger of another attack.

{Figure 03.04} Confederate soldiers from Laredo, Texas

Laredo was safe and Benavides rested until he regained his health. The Texas legislature passed a joint resolution that year that recognized Benavides' service:

> Be it resolved by the legislature of the State of Texas…that the thanks of the people are due and hereby tendered to Colonel Santos Benavides and the officers and men under his command for the steadfast opposition to the enemy in the field and the zeal they have shown in the service of their country…

For the rest of the war, Laredo remained in Confederate hands. In the summer of 1864, Colonel "Rip" Ford set off on a mission to regain control of the rest of the river.

Ford's 1864 Rio Grande Mission

After the Battle for Laredo, Union troop strength in the lower Rio Grande Valley began to decline considerably as troops were diverted from the region to other fronts. In June 1864, Colonel "Rip" Ford capitalized on the turn of events. With the help of Cristobal Benavides in Laredo, Ford led sixty men south along the river. After occupying Ringgold Barracks near Rio Grande City, he pushed on further south toward Brownsville. On the way there, Ford was joined by men from the 4th Arizona Cavalry. The additional troops raised his numbers to 250. Outdated reports informed Union Captain Phillip Temple that Ford still only had sixty men. Consequently, Temple, with 100 troops, made plans to surprise Ford before he arrived in Brownsville.

The two armies met at Las Rucias Ranch (about twenty-four miles west of Brownsville). At the conclusion of the short battle, Temple was decisively defeated. Out of his 100 men, twenty were killed, twenty-five were wounded, and thirty-six were taken prisoner. When the news reached Brownsville, Union commander Francis J. Herron evacuated Fort Brown. Fleeing Union troops (including members of the USCT) set up camp at Brazos Island, where they remained until the end of the war. The occupation of Fort Brown by Ford's troops in June of 1864 placed the lower Rio Grande Valley in Confederate hands.

Juan Cortina was now a general in the Mexican Army and the military governor of Tamaulipas. He wanted revenge against Confederate Texans for past grievances. So, he allied himself with the Union. In September of 1864, he suspended the cotton trade in Matamoros and Bagdad and opened artillery fire on Confederates from across the river. Although Union troops at Brazos Island had engaged Confederates in minor skirmishes, the threat that they posed for the cotton trade was minimal compared to Cortina's 1864 activities.

Juan Nepomuceno Cortina and the American Civil War

In July, 1864, Union Forces abandoned Brownsville, leaving Juan Cortina facing hostile Confederates to his north and equally hostile Austro-French imperialists advancing on Matamoros from the south. Cortina made plans to cross some 1,500 men of his Cortina Brigade to the north bank of the river where they could join Union forces. As many as 300 of Cortina's Exploradores del Bravo with three pieces of artillery did successfully cross the river on September 8, 1864, where they joined with Federal forces in an attack on Confederates near Palmito Ranch. In the fighting, twelve Cortinistas were captured and held as prisoners of war. The presence of the Cortinista army in the United States touched off a firestorm of diplomatic protests from the French.

After surrendering Matamoros and a brief stint in the Imperial Army, Cortina turned against the French in April 1865, and once again opened friendly relations with the Federals, who were holding Brazos Island and a sliver of the Rio Grande. With the conclusion of the Civil War, Cortina even opened a recruiting office in Brownsville. While on a tour of the Rio Grande frontier in the summer of 1865, General William Tecumseh Sherman met with Cortina in Brownsville and war materials began flowing into Mexico to support the Liberals and Benito Juarez in the bloody struggle against the Imperialistas. By late June 1866, the remnants of the once grand Imperial army evacuated Matamoros and Cortina rode triumphantly into the city. For years to come, as the Liberals fought one another for power in Mexico, Cortina continued to compete for the hearts and minds of the people of Tamaulipas and South Texas.

Excerpt from UTRGV Civil War Trail –University of Texas Rio Grande Valley

Ford, who had dealt with Cortina for years, evaluated his motivation:

> He hates Americans; particularly Texans. He has an old and deep-seated grudge against Brownsville. He knows his career is nearly closed. If he could force his way through our lines, plunder our people, and get within the Yankee lines, it would [be] a *finale* he would delight in.

> **Brownsville During the Civil War**
>
> Before and during the Civil War, Brownsville was a major hub in the international trade flowing out of the Rio Grande. Slavery was not common in Brownsville, so when the Civil War erupted, Brownsville residents chose sides for either personal or business reasons. When Texas seceded from the Union in February 1861, Confederates chased their Unionist neighbors out of town and confiscated their properties. Many of those Union supporters fled across the river to Matamoros and formed military units to fight their former neighbors. When Union ships blockaded the southern coastline, planters from Louisiana, Arkansas, and Texas shipped their cotton by train to the area south of Houston. From there, the "white gold" as cotton was known, was transferred by wagons on the difficult overland journey to Brownsville, where it could be ferried across the river to Matamoros. Mexico remained a neutral nation, so Union ships could not legally interfere with trade on the Rio Grande or in Mexican ports. By 1862, wagoneers lined up for miles along the road to Brownsville, waiting for their turn to stack their bales on the town's wharves. Hoping to stop the cotton trade, Union Army General Nathaniel Banks invaded South Texas in 1863. As Banks's troops burned Fort Brown and destroyed cotton cargoes, Unionists returned from Matamoros, reclaimed their property, and this time sent the Confederates rushing to the opposite shore. Military control of the city would change two more times in 1864. In May 1865, the Confederacy surrendered and Union forces, including US Colored Troops, reclaimed Brownsville.
>
> *Excerpt from UTRGV Civil War Trail –University of Texas Rio Grande Valley*

    Ford had no doubt that Cortina would cross the river and attack. Since Ford only had 300 men to defend Brownsville, he ordered his men to be constantly moving and changing their clothes to give Mexican scouts the illusion of greater Confederate numbers. Also, Ford made sure that Mexican scouts always saw him in the fort, so that an attack would not come because they believed that he had left. Ford and his troops spent some tense days and nights waiting for an impending attack. Fortunately for the Confederacy, Cortina's rule in Tamaulipas was short lived. Mexican Imperialist and French forces drove Cortina from Tamaulipas. Shortly after, Ford established cordial relations with General Tomas Mejia, the Imperialist commander of Tamaulipas, and the cotton trade was reopened.

End of the War

Union troops occupied Richmond, Virginia (the capital of the Confederacy) on April 3, 1865. On April 9, General Robert E. Lee surrendered to General US Grant at Appomattox Courthouse, Virginia. News of Lincoln's assassination swept through the nation less than a week after the events in Virginia. Lee's surrender put an end to most of the fighting east of the Mississippi. However, many Confederate leaders west of the Mississippi refused to accept defeat. In Texas, General John Bankhead Magruder (Confederate commander in Texas) asked Confederate troops to stand firm. On April 27, Texas Governor Pendleton Murrah challenged Texans "to redeem the cause of the Confederate government from its present perils." E. H. Cushing, the editor of the Houston *Daily Telegraph* called on Texans to continue to fight even if it meant resorting to "guerrilla warfare."

On May 8, the Union sent surrender terms to the Southern states that had still not laid down their arms. Governors from Louisiana, Arkansas, and Missouri met with a Texas representative (because the Texas governor was ill) at Marshall, Texas to discuss the document. The leaders rejected the terms (which were similar to the terms that Lee had accepted) and drafted their own proposal, which called for peace without a formal surrender. The Union rejected the Marshall Conference proposal.

{Figure 03.05} Battle of Palmito Ranch

On May 11, Colonel Theodore H. Barrett (commander of at Brazos Island) ordered 500 Union troops to march toward Brownsville. On May 13, Barrett was met by Colonel "Rip" Ford and 300 Confederate troops and artillery near Palmito Ranch (fifteen miles east of Brownsville). During a rainstorm, Barrett retreated and a bombardment by the Union Navy held Ford back long enough to allow the Union troops to escape. Several men were wounded and two Union troops were killed. (Some historians believe that the number of fatalities on both sides was much higher.) Private John Jefferson Williams of the 34th Indiana Infantry earned the unfortunate distinction of becoming the last battlefield fatality of the American Civil War.

A few days after the battle, several Union officers rode into Brownsville and met with General James E. Slaughter (commander of the Western Sub-District of Texas) and Ford to discuss a truce. During the discussion, Slaughter and Ford agreed that there was no point in continuing to fight. Ford released his men, and they went back to their homes. The Civil War was over in the lower Rio Grande Valley.

{Figure 03.06} Private John Jefferson Williams, the last casualty of the US Civil War

Chapter 4: Reconstruction (1866-1877)

Immediate Aftermath of the American Civil War

Although the war was over in the lower Rio Grande Valley, other Texas Generals sought to hold on in Galveston and Houston. However, they were unable to continue to fight, due to massive troop desertions. The collapse of military authority and the Confederate government resulted in widespread chaos and confusion. Riots broke out in several major Texas cities (including Houston, Galveston, Austin, and San Antonio) as armed returning troops claimed that they had not been paid. Warehouses and stores were looted to secure food. One Texan observed, "The army has entirely disbanded, & are sacking as they go.... We have no Govt. or country. God help us."

On June 2, 1865 (approximately two months after Lee's surrender), the war was officially over in Texas. As US troops arrived in the former Confederacy to restore order, many former Confederate political and military leaders fled the country. The governors of Louisiana, Missouri, and Texas, as well as several generals (including Magruder, Slaughter, and Bee), crossed the Rio Grande and settled in Mexico. Others (about 300) journeyed as far as Brazil and other parts of South America. Some of them returned after a few years, but others never returned. On June 19 (the "Juneteenth"), US General Gordon Granger arrived in Galveston with 1,800 troops and declared that the Emancipation Proclamation was in effect, and with General Order Number 3, he officially abolished slavery in Texas:

> The people of Texas are informed that, in accordance with a Proclamation from the Executive of the United States, all slaves are free. This involves an absolute equality of rights and rights of property between former masters and slaves, and the connection

heretofore existing between them becomes that between employer and free laborer. The freedmen are advised to remain at their present homes and work for wages. They are informed that they will not be allowed to collect at military posts, and that they will not be supported in idleness, either there or elsewhere.

The announcement presented African Americans with new challenges. After living in slavery for many years, the concept of freedom was difficult to grasp. Sarah Ford, a former slave, explained, "When freedom [came] I didn't know what [that] was." Before 1865, slaves were told what jobs to do and where to live. After the war, each former slave would need to find new answers to these questions. In 1865, the US Government established the Freedmen's Bureau to help former slaves find jobs and homes. In Texas, the Freedmen's Bureau created 150 schools for African Americans.

End of Mexican Civil War

The lower Rio Grande region was unstable after the war. Some feared that former Confederate leaders might return to the US and foment another Civil War. In addition, the Mexican Civil War was still raging and violence sometimes spilled over into South Texas. Also, Native Americans occasionally raided settlements in their quest for horses and other needed supplies. For these reasons, the US government sent three regiments of the United States Colored Troops (USCT) to guard South Texas. The 16,000 men were spread among Fort Brown (Brownsville), Ringgold Barracks (Rio Grande City), Fort McIntosh (Laredo), Fort Duncan (Eagle Pass), and several other smaller posts along the Rio Grande.

Throughout Reconstruction, the USCT made up the bulk of the occupation force in the Rio Grande Valley. The USCT built permanent brick structures at Fort Brown (which

{Figure 04.01} Fort McIntosh

had been partially destroyed by fire in 1863), Ringgold, and McIntosh. In addition, they built several smaller encampments between the main forts. By patrolling between these bases, the USCT maintained security in the region. They dealt with various threats to life and property including Native American attacks and cattle rustlers. However, the biggest threat that they faced was possible violence from Mexico. By the end of 1865, 50,000 US troops were stationed in Texas.

{Figure 04.02} Flag representing US Colored Infantry

> **US Colored Troops**
>
> Early in 1863, Abraham Lincoln observed: "The colored population is the great available yet unavailed of force for restoring the Union." Two months later the War Department issued General Order #143 which sanctioned the creation of the United States Colored Troops (USCT). Three regiments of the USCT entered the Rio Grande Valley in the fall of 1864. Encamped at Brazos Santiago, a detachment of the 62nd Infantry fought Confederates at the Battle of Palmito Ranch on May 13, 1865. Two weeks later, on May 30, the 62nd, along with other US Army units, moved into Brownsville. By May 1865, nearly 16,000 USCT veterans of the 25th Corps arrived at Brazos Santiago from City Point, Virginia, and were quickly dispersed to Forts Brown at Brownsville, Ringgold Barracks at Rio Grande City, Fort McIntosh at Laredo, and Fort Duncan at Eagle Pass, as well as to smaller posts where they were assigned to prevent former Confederates from establishing their defeated government and army in Mexico. Later, the USCT, along with their successors the "buffalo soldiers"—as they were called by Plains Indians—patrolled the border to stop ongoing violence in Mexico from spilling into the United States, and to discourage bandits and Indians from attacking civilian communities. The black soldiers made a fine adjustment to the diverse culture of the Valley, as explained by Sergeant Major Thomas Boswell of the 116th: "If our regiment stays here any length of time we will all speak Spanish, as we are learning very fast." The last USCT regiment, the 117th US Colored Infantry, left the Rio Grande in July 1867.
>
> *Excerpt from UTRGV Civil War Trail – University of Texas Rio Grande Valley*

By 1866, the Mexican Civil War was winding down as Juarez's forces gained the upper hand. As violence escalated during the final push to bring the war to a close, the US consul in Matamoros requested protection. During the chaos, Cortina once again presented a threat to the lower Rio Grande Valley when he declared himself governor of Tamaulipas. In response, the US sent troops to Matamoros consisting largely of USCT. The troops remained there until December 1, 1866. By then Napoleon III ordered Maximillian to give up the throne and return to Europe, but he chose to remain in Mexico. In April 1867, Juarez's forces liberated Mexico City. The execution of Maximilian and his generals in June brought the war of the French Intervention to an end. The end of the war in Mexico brought peace to the lower Rio Grande Valley, and the US greatly reduced its military presence along the Rio Grande. The last of the USCT mustered out of service in July 1867. That same year, a hurricane wiped out the port town of Bagdad. In its place, the storm left only sand dunes and marshland. Since that time, Bagdad only survived on old maps and history books.

{Figure 04.03} Buffalo Soldiers by Frederick Remington

Reconstruction

The US government declared all Confederate laws invalid. Texans had to reconstruct (or rebuild) the state government in order to be allowed to rejoin the Union. US President Andrew Johnson appointed Andrew J. Hamilton as governor of Texas in June 1865, and Hamilton's administration went quickly to work on a new state constitution, which was approved in 1866. Some African Americans participated in the new Texas government; some voted while others entered politics. Fourteen African Americans were elected to the Texas legislature. Matthew Gaines, who had been brought to Texas as a slave in 1854, was elected to the Texas Senate in 1869. George T. Ruby, who had come to Texas in 1866 as an agent for the Freedmen's Bureau, served as a state senator, president of the Texas Loyal Union League, and delegate to the Republican National Convention in 1868.

In 1860, Texas had about 182,000 slaves. Throughout the war, that number grew by about 30,000 as slave refugees from surrounding states were brought to Texas. According to historian Ralph A. Wooster, when emancipation came at the end of the war "Texas slaves greeted the event with joy." During Reconstruction, the US government added amendments to the US Constitution that formalized the new legal status of former slaves.

Before the war, slaves were not allowed to leave their masters. However, the Thirteenth Amendment (1865) ended (or abolished) slavery in the entire US. This meant that former slaves were now free to move around. This new freedom led to an important social change. Many slave families had been broken up and sold to several different masters; freedom of movement allowed these families to reunite. An important economic change had to do with wages. Before the war, slaves worked for their masters for no money. After slaves were set free, they had to find new ways to earn a living. During Reconstruction, many former slaves became sharecroppers (farmers who pay part of the crops they grow to a landowner).

During these years, governments in the Southern states were led by former Confederates. Some people felt that these leaders were not treating African Americans fairly. Even president Johnson, who was from Tennessee, received similar criticism. Consequently, in 1867 the US Congress took control of Reconstruction. Congress removed former Confederates from state governments and ordered that the former Confederate states be divided into military districts run by Union military commanders.

The Fourteenth Amendment (1868) brought about another important political change. It declared that all native-born or naturalized persons were citizens. The Fourteenth Amendment said that all former slaves had the right to be protected and treated equally under the law. Unfortunately, many people in the South ignored the Fourteenth Amendment. The black codes had a big social impact on the life of former slaves and their children, because these laws enforced segregation (kept people in separate groups based on their race). Segregation was enforced in all public places. Lynching (acts of violence and the hanging of former slaves) was also common. Congress responded by requiring all Southern states to accept the Fourteenth Amendment as a condition to rejoin the Union. As part of this requirement, Congress also required that Texas write a new state constitution that was aligned with national Reconstruction goals. The new Texas Constitution was approved in 1869. That same year, Texas voters elected Republican Edmund J. Davis governor. Davis supported African American rights.

The Fifteenth Amendment (1870), another important political change, declared that the right to vote should not be denied on the basis of race. Some white Americans opposed African American rights, and they resorted to acts of violence. During and after Reconstruction, many African Americans were beaten and killed. Due to the Fifteenth Amendment, former male slaves now had a legal right to vote, but some states in the South, including Texas, found ways around that requirement . Years after Reconstruction, the poll tax set a fee that people had to pay in order to vote. Many poor people could not afford to pay the tax, so they were not allowed to vote.

Some states made voters take literacy tests to prove that they could read. If they could not read, they were not allowed to vote. Many former slaves had never been to school, so they could not read. The threat of violence and these laws discourage many former slaves from voting.

However, not all African Americans shunned voting booths. Various groups continued to promote and celebrate African American rights. In 1866, the one-year anniversary of the Juneteenth, African Americans gathered to teach thousands of former slaves about their voting rights. Since that time, African Americans have continued to celebrate the Juneteenth in Texas and in other parts of the South. In fact, African American soldiers have held Juneteenth celebrations on military bases around the world. Thousands of people gather each year to hear speeches, enjoy music, and eat food prepared in cookouts. Friends and family members often hold reunions at the events.

End of Reconstruction

On March 30, 1870, President US Grant signed an act that readmitted Texas to the Union and ended Congressional Reconstruction in Texas. However, Governor Davis continued to enforce Reconstruction initiatives. Some white Texans opposed Davis's commitment to African American rights. They especially disliked Davis's use of a state police force to enforce martial law. Some Texans believed that Davis had grown too powerful, and that he was using his authority to force his views on Texans. Many more were dissatisfied with rising state taxes. In 1865, the state tax rate had been 15 cents on every $100 worth of property. By 1872, however, the tax rate had skyrocketed to $2 on every $100 worth of property. In spite of Davis's accomplishments (including building many new roads, improving frontier defense, and establishing a system of free public schools), he became extremely unpopular.

In 1872, Democrats won a majority of seats in the Texas legislature, and they immediately began dismantling Davis's power structure. They abolished the state police force and took away the governor's power to declare martial law. In 1873, Davis ran for re-election against Democrat Richard Coke, a former Confederate officer from Waco, Texas. Coke received almost twice as many votes as Davis (100,415 to 52,141). However, controversy over the election soon arose.

On January 5, 1874, the Texas Supreme Court in the case of *ex parte Rodriguez* declared the election illegal, because it had only been held on one day. The 1869 Constitution stated that "the polls shall be open for four days." The violation of Constitutional law was uncovered when Joseph Rodriguez was accused by authorities in Harris County of voting twice on two separate days. Rodriguez's attorneys argued that the Thirteenth Legislature's decision on March 1873 to set only one day for the election meant that Rodriguez's second vote was immaterial, since it had been cast on a day not authorized by the legislature.

Davis ordered the state militia to occupy the ground floor of the capitol to bar anyone from entering the building. Coke supporters were not deterred. They used ladders to climb to the second floor. Coke was inaugurated governor on January 15, 1874. Davis telegraphed President Grant with a request for federal troops. The US Attorney General wired back:

> Your right to the office of Governor at this time is at least so doubtful that he [President Grant] does not feel warranted in furnishing United States Troops to aid you in holding further possession of it.

Davis formally resigned the governorship on January 19, 1874. Coke's victory meant the end of Reconstruction in Texas. The new leadership adopted a new Texas Constitution in 1876, which greatly reduced the power of the governor. Without federal intervention or a state-level defender like Davis, African Americans lost many of their rights and freedoms. In 1877, Reconstruction ended in the US.

{Figure 04.04} Rio Grande Valley Civil War Trail highway sign

Conclusion

From the time of the Texas Revolution to the end of Reconstruction, this turbulent era in the history of the Rio Grande Valley, Texas, and the nation forms part of our American heritage. A close study of this region during this time period reveals a dramatic story replete with "ethnic tension, international intrigue, and the clash of colorful characters that mark the Civil War era in this region" (Rio Grande Valley Civil War Trail website).

More than 150 years after the last shot of the Civil War was fired at the Battle of Palmito Ranch, the important role that the Rio Grande Valley played during the war is often overlooked in general histories of the Civil War and even general histories of Texas. It is the hope of both the author of this book and the University of Texas Rio Grande Valley CHAPS program team that more people will grow to appreciate the South Texas stage in which significant Civil War era events transpired.

Chronology

1836
Texas won independence from Mexico; the Republic of Texas was formed

1845
Texas gave up nationhood to become a state when it was annexed by the United States

1846
Mexican American War began

1848
Mexican American War formally ended with the signing of the Treaty of Guadalupe Hidalgo between the United States and Mexico. The treaty set the southern boundary of South Texas at the Rio Grande

1850
Compromise of 1850 set the present western boundary of Texas

1859-1860
Juan Cortina and his forces raided points along the lower Rio Grande Valley

1860
Abraham Lincoln was elected US President

1861
February 1 – Texas State convention approved an ordinance of secession
February 8 – Confederate States of America (CSA) adopted a constitution
February 9 – Jefferson Davis was elected CSA President
February 16 – General Twiggs surrendered federal forts in Texas
February 28 – Texas voters ratified the ordinance of secession
March 2 – Convention passed an ordinance uniting Texas with the CSA
March 4 – Lincoln was inaugurated US President
March 16 – Convention removed Sam Houston from office
April 12 – Confederates fired on Fort Sumter (South Carolina)
April 15 – Massacre at El Clareño, Texas
May 21 – Skirmish at Redmond Ranch in Carrizo, Texas

July 2 – US Navy initiated blockade of Galveston, Texas

1862
August 16-18 – Union troops bombarded Corpus Christi, Texas
October 8 – Union troops captured Galveston, Texas
October 21 – Battle of Port Lavaca, Texas

1863
January 1 – Confederates recaptured Galveston, Texas
November 2-6 Union troops occupied Brownsville

1864
March 19 – Battle of Laredo
June 25 – Las Rucias Battle
July 30 – Confederates reoccupied Brownsville
September 6 – First Battle of Palmito Ranch; Union troops left Rio Grande Valley

1865
April 3 – Richmond, Virginia occupied by Union troops
April 9 – General Robert E. Lee surrendered at Appomattox Court House (Virginia)
April 14 – Lincoln was assassinated
May 12-13 – Battle of Palmito Ranch
June 2 – War was officially over in Texas
June 17 – Texas placed under Presidential Reconstruction
June 19 – Emancipation Proclamation in effect in Texas

1867
Texas under rule of Congressional Reconstruction; Bagdad was destroyed by a hurricane

1870
March 30 – President US Grant signed an act that readmitted Texas to the Union and ended Congressional Reconstruction in Texas

1877
Reconstruction ended in the US

Appendix I: Russell K. Skowronek

Protecting the Archaeological Record
Doing the Right Thing

Military historians are well acquainted with the nature of war. Defensive features from campsites to fortifications to trenches are tangible reminders of past sieges. In Germany, Turkey, and Canada there are still the walled cities of Rothenberg, Istanbul and Quebec. In the United States the seaward approaches to Savannah and Charleston are still "defended" by the battered remnants of Forts Pulaski and Sumter. Foundations and such earth features as trenches, redoubts, and earthworks are still visible features across Belgium and France from WWI and at sites from the American Revolution and Civil War such as Yorktown, Vicksburg, and Petersburg. At these, the easily lost detritus of everyday life from toothbrushes, buttons, buckles, shoes, food remains and munitions are found in moats, latrines, bombproofs, and in the fields between the lines of antagonists.

But what of more moving battles fought across open ground? These too leave evidence of a conflict but that evidence is limited to portable artifacts such as buttons, badges, bullets which are easily lost in the heat of battle. Human or animal casualties were removed from the field by compatriots or other non-human scavengers. Useable munitions were similarly retrieved. Yet, the small easily lost and later overlooked objects can, through their relative position to one-another, reveal the movement of troops providing a more nuanced and less biased picture of a battle. In the Rio Grande region, the two dozen battles fought over a two-decade period were of this ephemeral nature.

Battlefield archaeology was born in the 1980s at the Little Bighorn battlefield in Montana, the site of the 1876 defeat of Custer's 7th Cavalry. Archaeologists wielding metal detectors and using standard forensic approaches, including ballistic study of spent ammunition, were able to trace the movement of the troopers and their Native American foes across the battlefield. What emerged was a very different image of the battle then that was told over the previous century.[1] What made their job easier was

---
[1] (Scott and Fox 1987)

that the battlefield had been largely untouched since the summer of 1876. Portable artifacts by the thousand and some human remains were discovered where they had fallen a century earlier. Thirty years later these same techniques have been used to investigate other battlefield sites from the Mexican-American and Civil Wars with their success tempered by the condition of the archeological record. [2]

This objective source of information is diminished through the undocumented collection of artifacts. Some have compared this to the tearing of pages out of a history book and the resulting loss of knowledge. Leisure time has spawned a growing interest in the past. Television programs including "Antiques Roadshow" on Public Broadcasting, "American Pickers" on the History Channel, and the now cancelled "Diggers" on National Geographic bring the significance of historic material culture into America's living rooms. In the desire to own a piece of the past relic hunters collect those portable artifacts which are crucial to understanding battlefields and archaeological sites in general. Some have used metal detectors to hunt for bullets, buttons, and buckles on sites associated with the American Civil War. Since the 1960s Palo Alto and Palmito Ranch battlefields and the sites of Bagdad, Clarksville, and the military camp at Brazos Santiago have been adversely affected through undocumented collecting at these sites (Galloso 2016). Perhaps to assuage their conscience some have donated their curios to local (e.g., Museum of Port Isabel, Port Isabel; the Ladd Hockey Collections at the Museum of South Texas History, Edinburg) and regional (e.g., Texas Civil War Museum, Fort Worth) museums. Others are proudly displayed in shadow boxes or are kept in shoeboxes pending the demise of their owners. Of course, such activities are illegal on public property but that does not stop dedicated collectors. These concerns regarding sites from the American Civil War are also applicable to prehistoric sites. If you grew up living or working on a farm or orchard, or if you hunt and fish, chances are you, or someone you know probably found evidence of the ancient ancestors of the Coahuiltecans or other Indian peoples. If you have or do discover such things, be a good steward of these precious non-renewable resources, because once the information is gone it can never be recovered. Some of the following answers to frequently asked questions marked with an asterisk are presented courtesy of the Texas Historical Commission.

---

[2] Hacker 2003; Texas Historical Commission 2011

If I let an archeologist record or study an archeological site on my land, will I risk losing my property?

No. The Texas Historical Commission has no legal authority to acquire property through imminent domain. Texas Historical Commission regional archeologists work with landowners and can recommend voluntary actions to take to protect and preserve important sites. Protective measures, including designations and easements are most effective when landowners understand what archeological resources occur on their property and where they are located.

Will the government confiscate the artifacts I find on my property?

No. Artifacts from private land are the property of the landowner.

Who owns the materials?

In the United States, on private property the landowner is the owner of everything on their property, including archaeological materials. If you are on private land and you find something, do not pick it up without the permission of the landowner.

What if I am on vacation and find archaeological materials?

On public lands, including state and national parks, seashores, and historic sites **ALL** artifacts belong to the people of Texas and the United States. **NEVER** pick up artifacts on public lands. It is a felony. Do the right thing and inform rangers or interpreters of the discovery. Do NOT tell other people about the location of the site as they might not do the ethical thing and may illegally collect materials.

Why shouldn't I keep these items? There must be more.

Archaeological sites are non-renewable resources. Once an object is removed from a site its physical relationship to the other artifacts that make up the site is lost. If the diagnostic artifacts are all collected from a site we will never know the age or cultural affiliation of the site. In the case of Civil War era sites we will not have direct evidence of troop movements. We must remember that the documentary record is often incomplete or biased leaving only the archaeological record as the final arbiter of what happened in the past.

What should I do if I find or have found something on my property?

It is important to know exactly where each object was found. Recording the location of the discovery will allow future researchers to better understand its place in the past. Ideally, you will use your hand-held GPS unit to mark the location of the site. Another way is to use Google Earth images to exactly pinpoint the location of the site.
Be certain to write the location on the bag in which you store the artifacts and record it on a sheet of paper you place in the bag.

I have some artifacts I have collected over the years. Are they important?

Artifact collections have the potential to shed important light on the sites from which they were collected. An important factor is if artifacts from specific sites were labeled or kept separately from other site collections. If so, then archeologists can study and compare the collections with other artifacts retrieved from the same site or area. Collections that lack this information have either limited or no research value. While the artifacts may be interesting to look at, without identification and location information, they tell us little or nothing about past occupations at a specific locale.

What can I do to protect a site on my property?

If you are involved in crop agriculture, each disking or plowing episode will further mix the artifacts. Avoidance of the artifact concentration is preferred. Livestock can destroy artifacts and archaeological sites by trampling. Fencing would limit this impact. Finally, replacing trees or ditching for irrigation in orchards can also adversely affect a site. If avoidance is impossible, ask an archaeologist or an archaeological steward (see below) to monitor during digging. The Texas Historical Commission's (THC) Archeology Division has regional archeologists who can assist private landowners in identifying and recording archeological sites. Members of the THC's Texas Archeological Stewardship Network can also assist property owners. For assistance, contact the THC's Archaeology Division.

Why is that important?

Other materials found on your property might represent occupations dating from other eras. Should the materials become mixed, important information about all the sites will be compromised.

What should I do after I have found a site, not disturbed it and recorded its location?

If you live in Cameron, Hidalgo, Starr, or Zapata Counties, contact the CHAPS Program Office at the University of Texas Rio Grande Valley. We will photograph, identify, and record your site. ALL artifacts will be returned to the owner following analysis, along with a copy of our site report.

Are the artifacts valuable?

Archaeologists do not put dollar-values on artifacts. The value is in what they can tell us about the past. That is why it is imperative that the exact location or context of the discovery must be recorded. Artifacts without context are simply curios or curiosities.

Why should I care?

While individuals or their families may own land today in the future it will pass out of their hands. Some people act as stewards or protectors of their land to ensure it is not compromised. One family in Edinburg purchased a farm a century ago. In 2011, at their request, archaeologists discovered that other families had lived on that land for the previous eighty centuries. That information has now been recorded in perpetuity and can now be shared with interested researchers and future generations of residents in the region. When that property is sold and subdivided the unique information from this multi-component archaeological site will be preserved and will be forever known by the landowner's family name.

The Texas Historical Commission produces a number of useful brochures relating to these issues and others. Titles include *"A Property Owner's Guide to Archeological Sites," "Artifact Collecting in Texas," "Destruction of Archeological Sites in Texas,"* and *"Laws that Protect Archeological Sites."* These articles and other information on archaeology may be found at the Texas Historical Commission webpage at: **www.thc.state,tx.us**

References Cited:

Galloso, Robin L. 2016. Archaeological Potential of the Rio Grande Valley: A Look at Brazos Island with a Historical Focus on the Civil War. MA Thesis, Department of History, University of Texas Rio Grande Valley, Edinburg, Texas.

Haecker, Charles M. 2003. *An Historical Archeological Perspective of the Battlefield of Palmito Ranch, "…The Last Conflict of the Great Rebellion…".* National Park Service, Heritage Partnerships Program, Denver, Co. Report Produced for National Park Service American Battlefield Protection Program, Washington, D.C. ABPP Grant GA-2255-00-0002.

Scott, Douglas D. and Richard A. Fox, Jr. 1987. Archaeological Insights into the Custer Battle, An Assessment of the 1984 Field Season. University of Oklahoma Press, Norman, OK.

Texas Historical Commission. 2011. *Palmito Ranch Battlefield National Historic Landmark Final Technical Report with Archeological Survey Report: Grant Number: GA-2255-09-008.* Report Prepared for the National Park Service American Battlefield Protection Program. Washington, DC.

Appendix II: County Maps

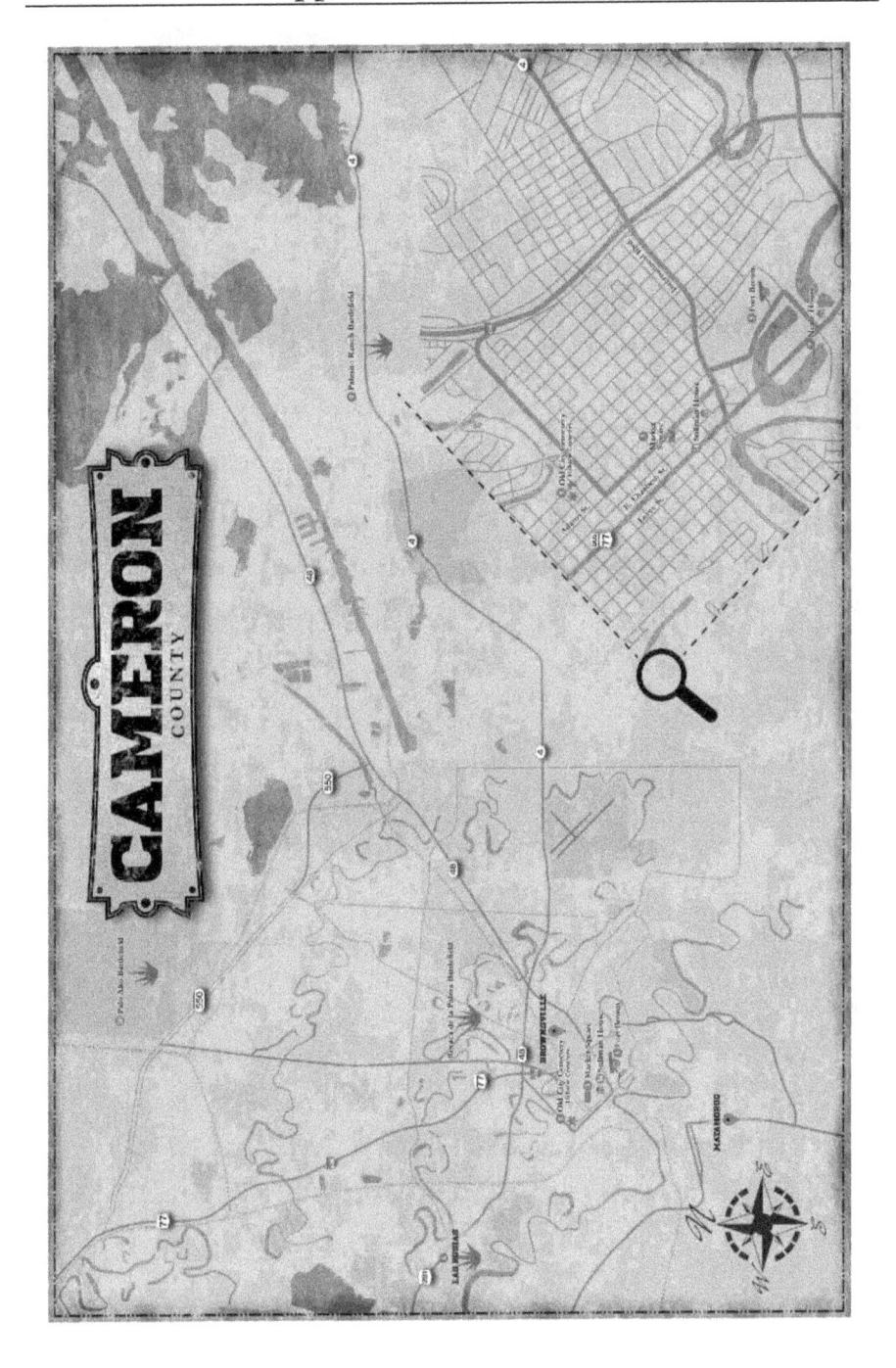

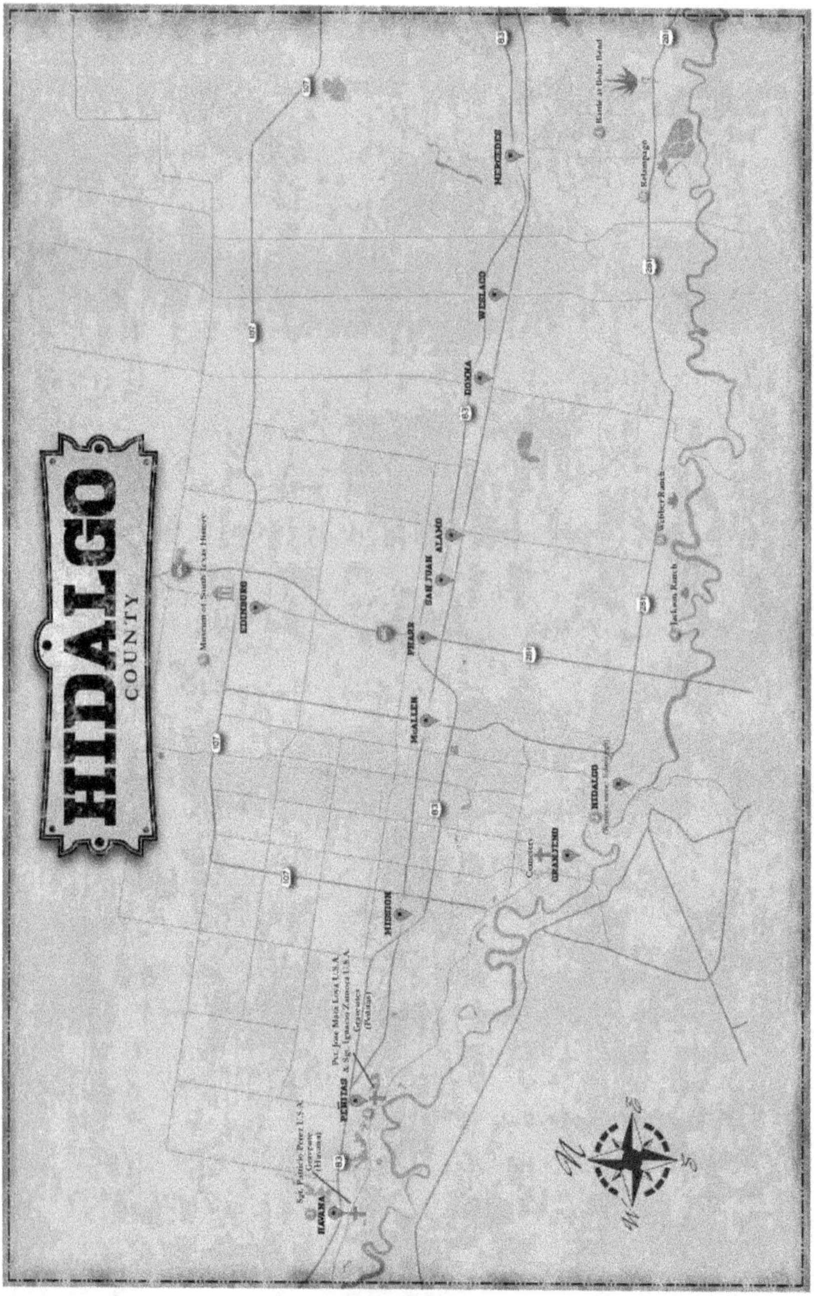
HIDALGO
COUNTY
Museum of South Texas History
EDINBURG
McALLEN
PHARR
SAN JUAN
ALAMO
DONNA
WESLACO
MERCEDES
MISSION
GRANJENO
HIDALGO
PEÑITAS
HAVANA
Jackson Ranch
Relampago
N
S
E
W

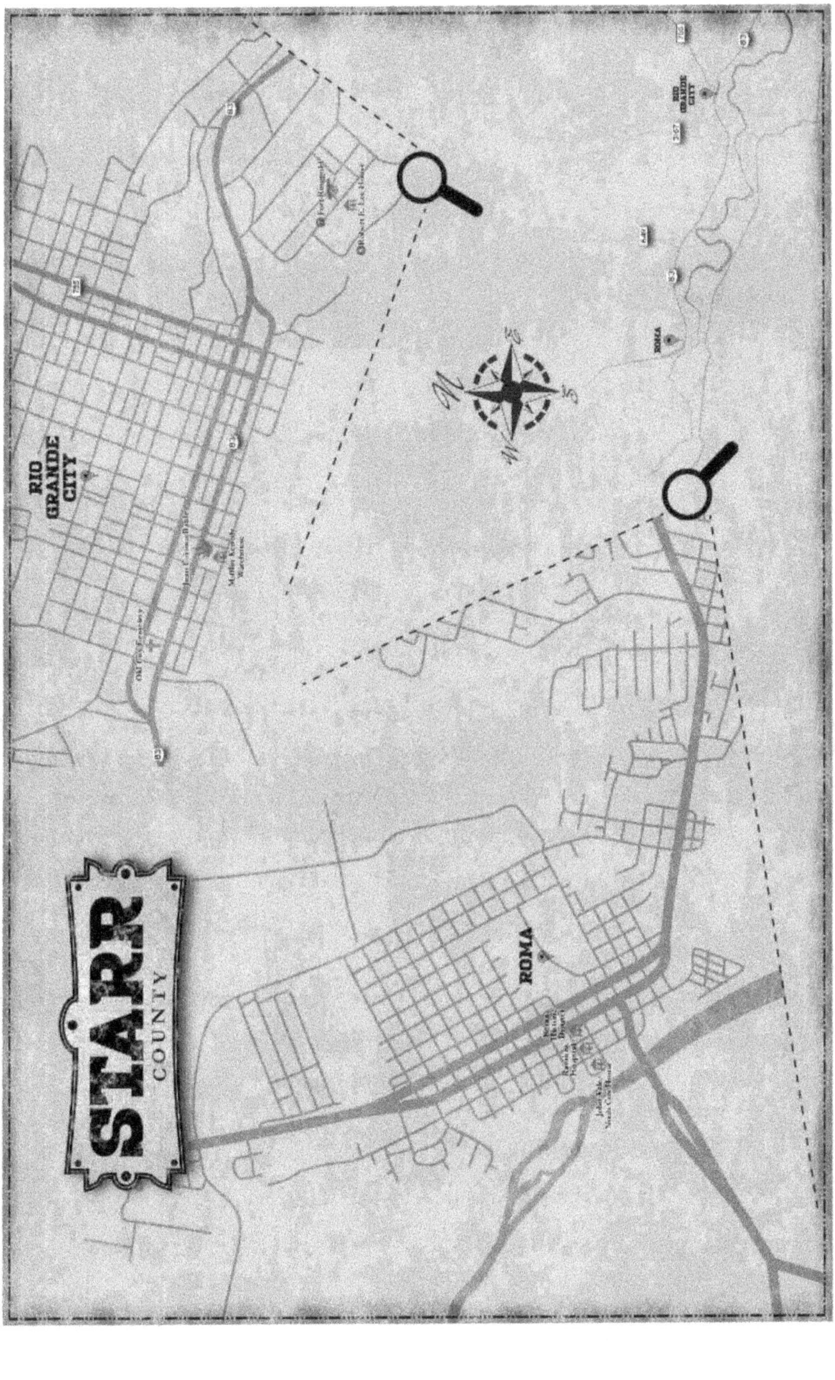
STARR
COUNTY
RIO GRANDE CITY
ROMA

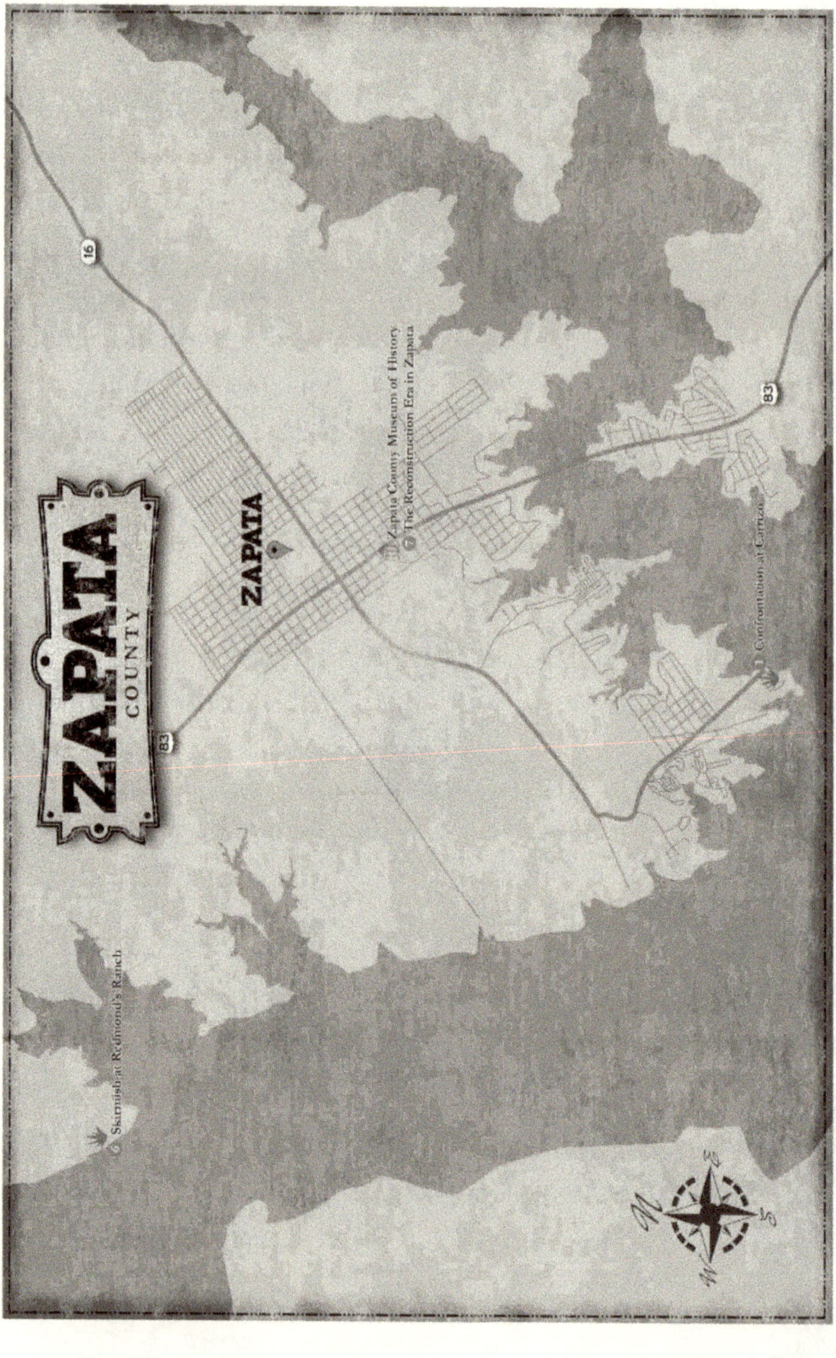
ZAPATA
COUNTY
ZAPATA
16
83
83
Zapata County Museum of History
The Reconstruction Era in Zapata
Confrontation at Carrizo
Skirmish at Redmond's Ranch
N
E
S
W

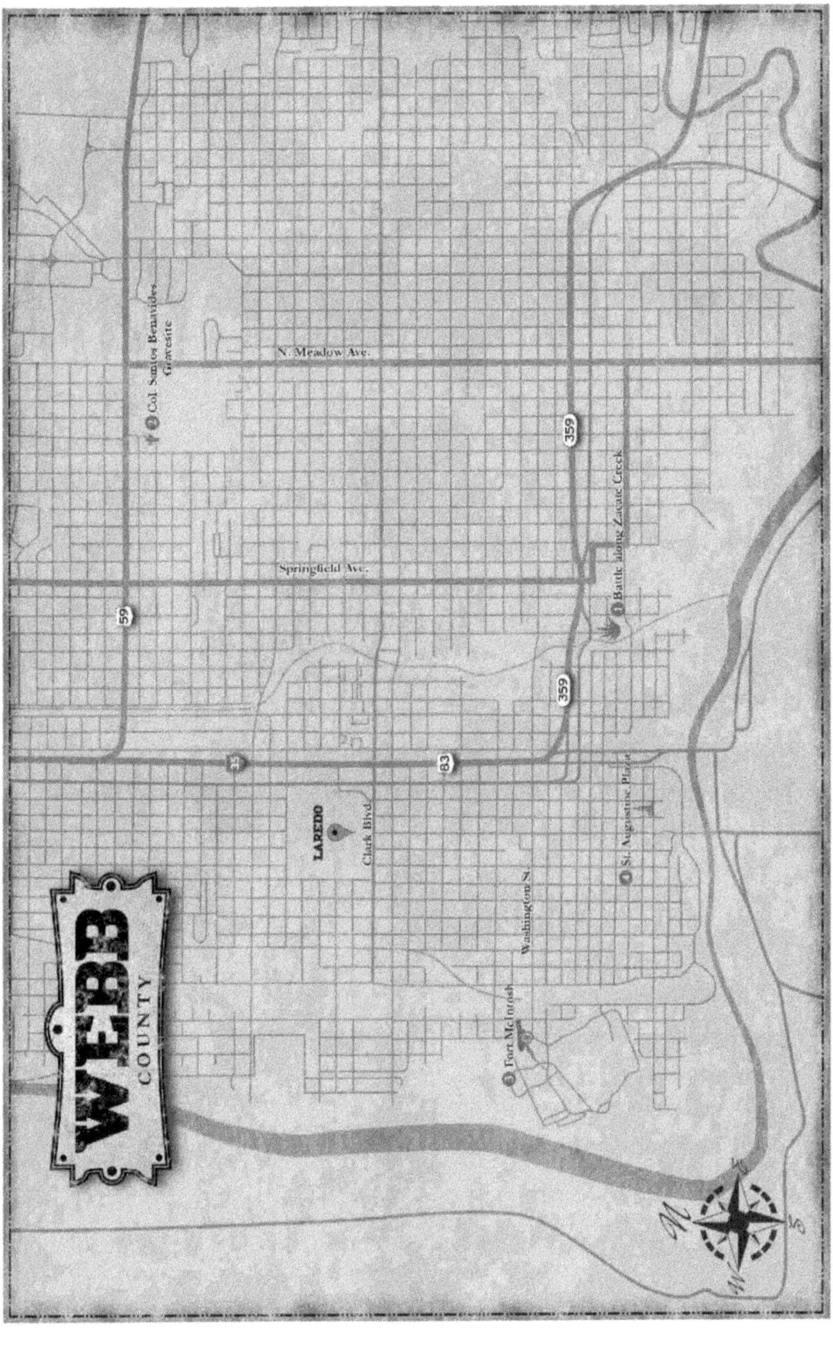
WEBB
COUNTY
LAREDO
Clark Blvd.
Washington St.
Fort McIntosh
St. Augustine Plaza
Battle along Zacate Creek
Springfield Ave.
N. Meadow Ave.
Col. Santos Benavides Gravesite
59
35
83
359

Further Reading

Books

Ahlstrom, Richard Mather. 2008. *Texas Civil War Artifacts: A Photographic Guide to the Physical Culture of Texas Civil War Soldiers.* Denton: University of North Texas Press.

Howell, Kenneth Wayne. 2009. *The Seventh Star of the Confederacy: Texas During the Civil War.* Denton, Texas: University of North Texas Press.

Hunt, Jeffrey William. 2002. *The Last Battle of the Civil War: Palmetto Ranch.* Austin, Texas: University of Texas Press.

Irby, James A. 1977. *Backdoor to Bagdad: The Civil War on the Rio Grande.* El Paso, Texas: Texas Western Press.

Leiker, James N. 2002. *Racial Borders: Black Soldiers along the Rio Grande.* College Station: Texas A&M University Press.

Owsley, Frank Lawrence and Harriet Chappell Owsley. 1959. *King Cotton Diplomacy: Foreign Relations of the Confederate States of America.* Chicago: University of Chicago Press.

Smith, Thomas T. 2000. *The Old Army in Texas: A Research Guide to the U.S. Army in Nineteenth-Century Texas.* Austin, Texas: Texas State Historical Association.

Thompson, Jerry D. 2017. *Tejano Tiger: Jose de los Santos Benavides and the Texas-Mexico Borderlands, 1823-1891.* Fort Worth, Texas: TCU Press.

_____. 2000. *Vaqueros in Blue and Gray.* Austin, Texas: State House Press.

Thompson, Jerry D. and Lawrence T. Jones, III. 2004. *Civil War and Revolution on the Rio Grande Frontier: A Narrative and Photographic History*. Austin, Texas: Texas State Historical Association.

Townsend, Stephen A. 2006. *The Yankee Invasion of Texas*. College Station, Texas: Texas A&M University Press.

Tucker, Phillip Thomas. 2001. *The Final Fury: Palmito Ranch, the Last Battle of the Civil War*. Mechanicsburg, Pennsylvania: Stackpole Books.

Wooster, Ralph A. 1999. *Civil War Texas: A History and a Guide*. Austin, Texas: Texas State Historical Association.

Articles

Marvel, William. 2006. "Last Hurrah at Palmetto Ranch." *Civil War Times*, 44 (6):66-73.

Noris, David A. 2016. "Showdown on the Rio Grande." *Military History*, (July):50-57.

Oates, Stephen B. 1963. "Texas Under the Secessionists." *The Southwestern Historical Quarterly*, 67(2):167-212.

Thompson, Jerry D. 1980. "A Stand Along the Border: Santos Benavides and the Battle for Laredo." *Civil War Times Illustrated*, 19(5):26-33.

Townsend, Stephen. 2007. "The 1864 Confederate Campaign against Brownsville." *Journal of South Texas*, 20(2):237-255.

Tyson, Carl Newton. 1975. "Texas: Men for War; Cotton for Economy." *Journal of the West*, 14(1):130-148.

Valdez, Joyce. 2001. "Hispanic Soldiers Played a Notable Role in the Civil War." *Hispanic*, 14(5):84.

Watson, Elbert L. 2009. "The Last Battle of the Civil War." *Traces of Indiana & Midwestern History*, 21(3):36-43.

Webpage
Rio Grande Valley Civil War Trail, http://www.utrgv.edu/civilwar-trail/

Index

American Civil War
    Anaconda Plan 31-32
    End of war 50-52
    Immediate Aftermath 54-55
    Secession 23-28
    Shortages 30-31
    Start of war 23-28
Battle for Laredo 41-46
Brownsville during the American Civil War 49
Colonel Santos Benavides 42
Ford's 1861 Rio Grande Mission 28-29
Ford's 1864 Rio Grande Mission 47-50
Jackson Ranch 15
Juan Nepomuceno Cortina
    And the American Civil War 48
    First Cortina War 15-18
    Second Cortina War 27
Juarez, Benito 34
Mexican American War
    Palo Alto Battlefield 12
Mexican Civil War
    European Invasion 33-35
    End of war 55-58
Reconstruction 53-63
Republic of Texas 5-8
Rio Grande (in 1862) 35-38
St. Augustine Plaza 43
State of Texas 8-10
US Colored Troops (USCT) 40, 47, 55-58
Union Occupation 40-41
US Presidential Election (1860) 18-21

About the Author

Rolando Avila holds a Master of Arts degree in History and a Doctorate in Education from the University of Texas-Pan American. He is Lecturer of History at the University of Texas Rio Grande Valley. His research areas of interest include the American Civil War, South Texas, and American Education. Avila has published many Civil War and Education related articles and book chapters. His most recent books are *Lincoln and the Bolts of War* (2018) and *Rio Grande Valley Civil War Trail: 56 Lesson Plans* (2018).

Additional copies of this book can be ordered at www.lulu.com.

For more detailed coverage of the Civil War in the Rio Grande Valley, please see:

>Miller, Christopher L., Russell K. Skowronek, and Roseann Bacha-Garza, *Blue and Gray on the Border: The Rio Grande Valley Civil War Trail*, College Station: Texas A&M Press, 2018.

>Bacha-Garza, Roseann, Christopher L. Miller and Russell K. Skowronek, *The Civil War on the Rio Grande: 1846-1876*, College Station: Texas A&M Press, 2019.

For further educational tools and information on the Civil War in the Rio Grande Valley, go to our dedicated website and our mobile website:

www.utrgv.edu/civilwar-trail	http://paal.oncell.com